DATING BASICS 101

What Every Guy Should Know but Often Doesn't

David Linares

Order this book online at www.trafford.com
or email orders@trafford.com

Most Trafford titles are also available at major online book retailers.

Printed in the United States of America.

ISBN: 978-1-4907-0803-4 (sc)
ISBN: 978-1-4907-0840-9 (hc)
ISBN: 978-1-4907-0802-7 (e)

Trafford rev. 07/12/2013

 www.trafford.com

North America & international
toll-free: 1 888 232 4444 (USA & Canada)
fax: 812 355 4082

The old saying that
"behind every great man is a great woman"
is true, or in my case, many great women.

Contents

Preface

"To change our lives we must first change our minds."
~ Unknown

The secrets in this book were very difficult to write about. Not because the issue of dating is complex, but because the information was so hard to come by. As a therapist, I also struggled for a long time about how to best go about writing this information down. I wanted it to do more than just teach the "do's" and "do not's" of dating. You can pick up any magazine and find that kind of information every week in grocery stores across the world. I also struggled with my conscious. Many times in my life, I have passed on what I know about dating and women to seemingly nice guys, only to see some of them turn into pigs that use women for sex and money. As a therapist you can imagine how much that displeases me. It took some time and soul searching on my part to realize that I am not responsible for how knowledge is used. I realized that men who use women have often been starved for love for so long that once they could get it, they sometimes go a little nuts and get greedy, gorging themselves like pigs, and sometimes mistake lust for love.

I think of it like this, imagine you're stranded alone in the middle of a barren desert. No food, no water. You're dying in everyway. You body is not getting its nutritional or physical needs. Your mind is not getting any social stimulation (you're stranded alone, remember). Emotionally you are just about to give up hope of any chance of survival when—*bam!*—up from desert sands appears a huge table with all kinds of yummy foods and drinks and a pretty little waitress too. You'd better believe you're going to stuff your face with food and drink and savor every last bit of company you can get with the waitress. I realize there are a lot of potential dirty jokes to be made in this story. The point is it is just human nature to be greedy and overdo it when you are starving. If you picked up this book, the odds are you are not getting your physical or social needs met, and you just might be running out of hope too.

I don't want you to get greedy, but I do want you to be happy! Picking up this book and reading it shows a willingness (and intelligence) to change your life for the better. I recognize that asking for and being willing to seek change is not easy. I have always thought that it takes a stronger person to ask for help than for that person to try to do (whatever he or she wants to do) in life alone. Together we will work on changing how your mind works, and use the facts, tips, and tactics in this book to help you change your life to get what you want! As a bonus, you can avoid the embarrassment and drama that come with learning things the hard way. Life is hard enough as it is, so why add to the drama of it? Let this book save you the effort, the embarrassment, and the pain of learning the hard way.

For me the decision to write a book was made when a female friend of mine complained one day about a guy who she had just met and had called her five times in one day. *If you don't know, that is way too many times to call a girl after you meet her.* The guy turned out to be a friend of mine who I will refer to as "Fred." Fred was a twenty-three-year-old man who was tall and one of those annoying, overly healthy six-pack-abs kind of guy. He was by most people's measures a decent looking guy. My female friend had told Fred to buzz off on the fifth phone call. Then guess what happened. He came running to me for the first time asking what he did wrong. Some guys can be that clueless, and if that is or was you, don't worry. Everyone has to start from somewhere.

How sad, I thought, that my friend, at his age and with his fitness level, had still not figured out how to get and keep a girl's interest. My female friend confessed to me later she could have answered her phone any of the five times Fred called, but she wanted him to "work for it". Poor Fred *worked* himself right out of his chances with her. Clearly my friend liked him on some level when they first met or *she would not have given him her phone number.* She was playing a game with Fred and Fred, sadly as they say, had no game. *Just another example,* I thought *of how nice guys, the world over get treated like this and make simple but devastatingly costly mistakes.* I kind of had to figure that at Fred's age, this couldn't have been the first time he made a mistake like this. That meant for some reason Fred was not learning from his mistakes. Make no mistake about it: this was a simple, one time mistake that was devastating for Fred. Not only did it cost him his chance with my friend, but you can be sure my female friend went around telling all her friends about his obsessive calling. That made him look bad to women he might have had a shot with in the future.

This one little story in my life forced me to see that I can't just help out people I run into in my everyday life or who seek me out professionally. Fred had shown me that the problem of how to find a girl, get a date, and get into a relationship were not ones that everyone could just grow out of and learn naturally. If I was going to do this right, I figured I would have to reach out and teach people in a way that is accessible to everyone. Few, if any, methods beat writing a book. After all, as a young man myself, I would read book after book on all subjects about romance and dating. I did this for years and for years I put the knowledge I gained to the test by trial and error, discovering a few things no one warned me about along the way. While in college getting my degree in psychology, my main interest was in couples, marriage, and family therapy. So while there and in those classes, I also picked up on several important points from the basic to the advanced for all human relationships, paying notable interest and attention to topics relating to dating and relationships. All that work was paying off for me in ways I never expected. People noticed how often I was dating and started coming up to me asking how I do "it." I got asked just about every kind of relationship question you can think of from both sexes.

Statistically speaking, if you're reading this, you're a guy, so the book is written for the male reading audience. The book is written from a humanistic point of view, meaning that much of what is discussed is true and relevant for both males and females alike. From one guy to another, I want to tell you that if your lady ever finds this book and gets upset over it, don't panic. Just tell her the truth. You were having a hard time meeting someone like her and wanted something that would help with that. In a way, this book follows the same idea as all those girl magazines on the grocery store shelf that she and other girls buy. That's all you really need to say.

This book does of course go beyond anything you can get out of a magazine. "To first change your life you must first change your mind", a proverb that nicely summarizes this book. This book is designed to teach not just skills, or facts, but also a philosophy or way of life in how to view yourself and the world, particularly in the world of dating. What you will find in this book is useful information that works. Many so-called dating books are written for and only seem to work for a certain kind of guy who wants to date a certain kind of girl. Really "good" dating books will tell you *what* to do in a situation to get the girl but not *how* to do it. In short and at their best, other dating books seem to teach you how to date only a small portion of the female population. This book will teach you how to date a range of women regardless of who you are or what you look like.

To tell you bluntly, I wanted to avoid writing a "how to get laid book" for many reasons. First, such books are shallow and designed to build you up with false bravado. Second, they don't make you a better person. Third, they often don't teach you how to have real confidence in yourself and with women. Fourth, they often tell you how to do something without telling you *why* it works. I think it is extremely important to understand why things work because then *you can adapt, change, and modify what you learn, to fit who you are as an individual.* This is critical because obviously everyone is different. You need something that will work for you as an individual. You can then make "it" work for you in any situation and in any place. Fifth, just talking about how to get laid won't necessarily tell you a thing about what to do on the first, second, or third date and all the dates after, much less provide you with a basic foundation for building and maintaining a relationship. This book will provide you with all that and more.

I have no doubt that some people will look down on this book as a "how to get laid book." It was not my intention, and yet in my mind it is kind of a *must* for any good dating book. After all, the reality of life is that once you get a date and/or get laid (the two don't have to go hand in hand) you are naturally more liked by a woman and more likely to get sex. Also, I felt that trying to avoid giving you such information would be wrong on my part. I didn't think it would be fair or right of me to only half prepare you for dating and the possibility of sex. After reading this book, chances are extremely high that you are going to run into a girl who doesn't want to wait to have sex with you until you're married, and chances are you might be one of those guys who doesn't want to wait either. In the spirit of keeping this book real and at a human level as something that's useful to all men, I have included a bit of that information here and trust you as a reader to wisely use the knowledge you will gain.

How to help you gain that knowledge in a simple and easy manner was a big question on my mind when one day it just dawned on me that the best way to approach the subject of dating was in a real A-B-C, 1-2-3 kind of way. By that I mean everything starts within you and with your thoughts. So naturally we should start inside your thoughts, your beliefs, and your philosophy toward women and dating. This will dramatically change your outlook on life, dating, and women by bringing old and new ideas to the conscious mind. The added benefit is it will build on your own self-understanding, understanding of people, and most importantly your confidence with women. From there we will move outward to give you real practical knowledge and skills that are effective in meeting and dating women.

It may seem to you that such a small book as this couldn't really do all this for you. After all, the subject of dating seems so huge that entire volumes are written and dedicated to it. It is, however, a deception. It is a complex issue, but it is not *that* complex regardless of how you look, how old you are, or how lousy you are at dating. Simply knowing the basics and a few sound skills are all you need. Just keep it simple. It is when we get bogged down in the details of our own lives, lost in our problems and insecurities, and fail to see the human side of a situation that we get off track and make things complicated. It is kind of like that saying, "All I really needed to know I learned in kindergarten." All you really need to know are the basics and a few other minor things. The rest tends to fall into place naturally.

I do want to give a special note of thanks to my friends and patients who have shared with me what they have tried and learned in their own readings, teachings, and personal experiences. I recognize that some of the material contained within these pages may be found in other books or sources as I attempt to write about what I see as universal truths and currently popular cultural dating tactics. However, no actual text was consulted or intentionally reproduced in any way in this writing. Nonetheless, a silent nod of appreciation is given to those in the world who have come before me and spread the word of equality and shared the skills and knowledge of their own hard-earned trials and errors to ease the suffering of the lonely and broken-hearted.

My overarching goal is simple. I want to give the guys out there in the world the tools, knowledge, and skills to improve their lives, well-being, and relationships. This book will take you from A-Z on just how to do it. I want to enlighten you on how to do this. I'm tired of seeing people struggling to meet someone, being unwilling and unhappy twenty-something virgins, and ruining relationships that could have worked out. In short, to bring you a sense of happiness in your lives is my goal. It's critical to me that you understand what I am teaching you here is not to become something you're not, but rather to build on your awareness, confidence, and dating skills to the point of mastery. This is done by practicing and adding these skills to your knowledge base.

The end of your old life is here. Read on to start your new life!

CHAPTER 1

This Book Above All Others

"If you do not change direction, you may
end up where you are heading."
~Lao Tzu

A General Warning

I like the above quote because it basically means you might not like where you are heading if you don't change things up a bit. In a perfect world, you could easily meet someone who doesn't have any hang-ups. In a perfect world, you could meet someone, have this instant connection, and just fall in love because you are soul mates. The problem is, and I think you will agree, it's not a perfect world. The truth is you have to get out there and figure out who you are and what kind of person you're looking for. The fact is there are nearly seven billion people on this planet and not everyone meets someone to fall in love. I am even willing to bet a pretty high number of people die without ever having sex, much less finding love in a short-term or lifelong relationship. Don't let yourself unwittingly and unwillingly become one of these people.

Dating is hard, for men especially. Even the ugliest girl can get laid by a decent-looking guy if there's enough alcohol in him. But what happens when we reverse the story? The ugly guy is going to have to buy a lot of drinks and hope that the girl's friends don't keep him from getting her. Dating is hard, and nice guys normally finish last. Worse, the nice guys not only finish last, but often get stepped on, used, and disrespected by women who don't respect them. The number one reason this happens is because those nice guys often don't respect themselves. Let's say that women don't mean to be mean or to tease nice guys. Let's say sometimes a woman is just not a very sexual person, afraid of sex, or uncomfortable with her body. Believe it or not, there are people out there who don't like sex at all! Then there are the dirty, underhanded things people do. Perhaps she is just going out with you while she waits for someone better to come along or for her current boyfriend to get back to town. Perhaps she intends to introduce you to her boyfriend to make him jealous (this has happened to me more than once). Perhaps she says she wants to be your *friend* (translation: you buy everything) but the second you try to express your feelings or make a move on her she's gone like the Road Runner in a puff of smoke, and so is your so-called friendship.

Situations like these are just the tip of the iceberg when it comes to problems in dating. Perhaps you ask her out, but she's afraid of looking cheap and wants you to ask one more time. Another possible issue is that women, like men, can have low self-esteem, leading them to dump you because they don't feel able to be in relationship with nice guys or think you're cheating on them. So they go for the jerks or bums that treat them like they feel.

The psychology of the human mind, our personalities and how we interact, and what we expect from other people, particularly in relationships, is extremely complex. Other reasons that doom a meaningful relationship include, but are not limited to; people being drug addicts, heavy drinkers, gold diggers looking for the bigger better deal (also known as the BBD), and/or women looking to get married (because it is what society or the church expects of them). It could even be that a woman is afraid to get married and so dating a nice *"marrying"* guy is out of the question. Perhaps she just wants to get back at her parents, and bringing home a nice guy isn't going to do that. Perhaps life has been hard on her and she is emotionally unavailable. Whatever the possible reason, the bottom line is that girls, like men, have their hang-ups. Those hang-ups often get in the way of love.

I didn't major in philosophy; I can't tell you what love is. Is it something that develops out of lust? Out of playing the game? Or is it something else? Is love that instant connection you have when you see someone? Is it a choice we make like picking out some item in a store—we just pick one and go with it? Is it about settling, being happy with what you have and compromising on those little things that bug us about the person we're with?

Once you've had your fill of love and/or lust, I think you will find yourself in a place to decide for yourself what love is for you. What I can tell you is that if you believe and feel that you love someone, and she loves you back equally or greater, and if you feel a soulful connection without having to put up with mind games, then be smart. Don't do anything to let her down or hurt her if you can help it. A relationship like that is typically a once in a lifetime find. You will recognize that kind of relationship in part when the person you love tells you what she is thinking and feeling without any hesitation and when she takes good care of you, asking for very little or nothing in return.

What I'm going to do is teach you how to get past your issues, and most importantly, how to get past hers so you can get what *you both* want. That is right I said: *both*. Both you and your future lady (and just about every person on the plant) want to date, fall in love, and be happy. With this in mind, some of the stuff you're about to learn can be seen as underhanded and/or manipulative, but the truth is it's not. It's just not, and I will defend this no matter how hard someone tries to argue against it. The bottom line in my mind is that people want to be treated in a particular way in life and in certain situations. Some other people have defensive walls that are so high and so thick that no man could ever climb them or break them down. The alternative is to simply go around them or dig under them. What you are going to learn is something that everyone should learn and applies to nearly all people in all situations. While this book addresses so many aspects of dating, one major goal of the book is to teach you how to date *smarter*. In early 2010, the divorce rate in the United States changed from 50 percent of marriages ending in divorce to 60 percent of marriages now ending in divorce. This might be an indicator that people need to date smarter before marriage.

Remember that being single is simple. It's when we start coupling up that things get complicated. If you're in for the thrill of dating and/or love, and are in a place where you want to complicate the hell out of your life in wonderful ways, then read on.

The Process of This Book

As you progress in this book, we will go over how to have confidence in yourself, how to approach people, and how to "seal the deal" while applying homework lessons in each of these areas. I know homework sounds lame, but after all, friend, learning how to do something means absolutely nothing if you do not know how to use or do it properly. In other words, you will be learning how to use the proper tools for the proper job to get the desired outcome. I had a few reservations about the format of this book but ultimately stuck to the theory that a person can only read and truly understand so much information at a time. For this reason, the book's subjects and topics are occasionally repeated or elaborated on in other chapters so that you can reflect on them and hopefully understand them better. Even though I have chunked the information down for you in a way that I currently believe is best for learning, I do recommend that you read only one or two chapters a week. Then spend the rest of the next week working on and thinking about what you read for a minimum of one to two hours a day. This way you will be able to really understand what you are reading at a deeper level.

In this book, self-assessments and lessons are designed to seamlessly blend in your own personality traits and specific life situation for results!

I highly encourage you to highlight bits of information in this book. It will make reviewing the information faster and easier for you down the road. Take handwritten notes if you need to. Practice makes perfect and you will want to complete the few assignments in this book to help you remember the tricks, tip, and tactics to show real results!

Each chapter starts off with the chapter number followed by the main topic of that chapter. The subject of what each section found in that chapter will be is italicized so you can easily find any chapter and section you may want to reread. I also change up the wording used to describe females in the book to add more flavor to the reading and to reflect the different age ranges of females and the vocabulary used to describe them from one part of the world to the next. Sometimes I refer to women as women, and other times I will refer to them as ladies or girls.

CHAPTER 2

Cognitive Appraisals and You

"Knowing others is wisdom, knowing yourself is enlightenment."
~ Lao Tzu

The Faulty Mind

What's a cognitive appraisal? Simply put, it is how you think or feel about something, including yourself. Oftentimes our appraisals can be faulty, hence the *faulty mind* title of this chapter. In this chapter we are going to examine some commonly held thoughts and beliefs that affect your attitude toward members of the opposite sex. Our goal here is to look and see if you have any faulty thoughts floating around in your head that prevent you from getting what you want. Faulty thoughts may come from the teachings our parents, friends, movies, or social media. It is not critical to understand how faulty thoughts got into our head, only to correct them.

It is often the case that when we approach someone we want to get to know, we often become uncomfortable and even nervous. This can affect us so much so that we end up saying something stupid or worse, nothing at all. At least if you say something stupid you can play it off as a joke or an attempt at a joke. So how do we keep ourselves from being uncomfortable or nervous and avoid saying something that is less than ideal?

First thing you are going to do is sit back, relax, and think. Why might you be nervous around someone? Is it something within you? Are you embarrassed about how you dress? How you look? Your hairstyle? Are you afraid of being rejected? With all the different kinds of people out there, you shouldn't be.

Think about it. You sometimes see an ugly guy holding hands with a hot girl and probably have seen a short guy or girl dating a much taller person. Things like that just don't matter. Often we see what seem to be mismatched couples, but have you wondered what caused them to get together? Perhaps one or both of them were born with the intuitive knowledge on how to go about meeting someone. Perhaps they had modern-day Casanovas for fathers who instructed them on how to meet people. Casanova, in case you don't know, was a renowned lover of women in Italy in the 1800s. Perhaps they read a book like this one or even this same one, or took a class along the lines of this book. Perhaps they were just lucky. Regardless, together we will explore how to turn you into a modern-day Casanova through a step-by-step process.

Oftentimes we feel nervous around ladies it is because we have placed them automatically on a mental pedestal. Just the very act of approaching someone and trying to talk to her has you tipping your hand a bit, letting her now that there is something about her that you like. So your poker face is already failing you, buddy. How do we counteract this? To counteract this, we have to start before you ever see the person you want. You have to start with your beliefs. The faulty mind believes that women are different from us men. Other than physical differences, this is not true. They have thoughts and feeling the same as any male. What can help reduce your fears and counter your fearful behaviors is a philosophical change of attitude.

The world is a big place and, truth to tell, most of the world pretty much sucks when compared to the comforts that you and I have. Back in the orient, Buddhism started out as a philosophy, not a religion, and as a philosophy it put forth the idea that all life is suffering. This does not mean that life is all bad. It only means that everyone in life, no mater how rich, poor, or beautiful—*everyone, everywhere*—suffers. How does the rich man suffer? Well, for starters, he could be overly concerned that girls like him only for his money or worry about losing his money. You can imagine how much suffering such thoughts of fear and doubt on those two things alone can affect him in his everyday interactions with people and even late at night when he is alone. The same line of thought can be applied to the pretty girl. Are you interested in her for who she is on the inside or just her body? The pretty girl worries about her looks fading, about not being seen as smart, and always being perceived as the stupid, but pretty girl. These are just some of the specific thoughts that girls can worry about and suffer from. It is for this reason that one of the most effective ways to stand out from other guys is not to compliment a pretty girl on her looks, but rather to ask her what she *thinks*. This line of thought that I have explained doesn't even take into account the day-to-day worries or suffering that every human being must go though in life. Naturally, on the flip side, the unattractive or poor person may think that no one will ever love him or her or he or she is unworthy of love.

Take a moment to think of all the hardships you have had to go through in your life, everything you have suffered from. Well, guess what? No matter whom you talk to, they have suffered and had their own hardships too! Some people have had more suffering in their lives than others, but from the individuals' perspectives they suffered too. What's this mean? It means that we as human beings can only ever really experience our own suffering. Everything else that we gain from another person's story or perspective is just empathy, sympathy, or pity that we can feel for others. It is from understanding this that you need to realize that while you are dealing with your own issues, your own suffering, and, yes, even your own fears of rejection, so are they! No matter how great or confident or just plain hot a woman looks, I guarantee she has suffered in life and that means she is no better or worse than you.

When it comes to some women and suffering, it's possible that they may be suffering and struggling with their past, such as Daddy was never home and gave them no attention so now they seek it from men constantly. Perhaps they are suffering currently with some situation like their mom being in a hospital. Bottom line, you may not know how they are suffering, but both you and every person on the planet is suffering. What breaks up those moments of suffering with things like fear, doubt, worry, regret, and shame are the happy moments in our lives. Happy moments may include the birth of a baby, our birthdays, our favorite weekly television shows, our friends, hobbies, and family. What makes us happy depends on our point of view. For instance, our birthday could be a happy day or it could remind us we are one year older and perhaps one year closer to death. It's your point of view that determines how you see and feel about others, including yourself. Additionally, there is a set range of human emotion and it does not matter if you are boy or girl. We are all the same. The only difference is our bodily parts and how we perceive the world. This is the human condition and what makes you and every other person on the planet the same.

So how do you get over all that shyness, adopt a positive attitude, and feel more comfortable around members of the opposite sex? You just started. Just by thinking about the concept of suffering, you have started to realize that regardless of race, religion, or gender, all people are the same in this regard. This means that the hot girl across the room is more like you than you think, and this evens the playing field a bit. I recommend you go out and buy a book or two on Eastern philosophy, preferably on Buddhism or Taoism, to fully round out your understanding of this concept and others like it.

I'd be willing to bet that along with a lack of understanding that no matter how hot the girl you are interested in is, she's still human. There is also still the fear of being rejected. By understanding the concept of suffering you lessen the fear of rejection a bit (but I doubt you completely lose it). Do not worry because this is addressed a lot more in other chapters, but first things first. Another aspect of a faulty mind can be found in what we as men think our odds are of getting a girl. Being afraid she is to hot for you, taken, or somehow otherwise unavailable is one aspect of a faulty mind that can and often does prevent men from even trying. One of things you can do to possibly counter this fear is to start assessing your living situation. No, I am not taking about if you still live with your mom or how messy your place is. I am talking about the demographics of the area you live in. If you go to the United States Census Bureau and look up your local area, you can find information on your local population. Specifically, you can look for the ratio of men to women in your town. This is useful for several reasons. First, if you are in a place where men significantly out number girls, of course your odds of meeting someone who is single goes down a bit. On the other hand, if you live in a place where women significantly outnumber the men, finding a single girl is more likely. Secondly, this information is useful because it tells you how competitive you have to be. If you are in a high female area you won't have to do a lot to get a girl. This also means you don't have to be as concerned about rejection. Even if you are in a low female area, your fear should be less because now you know your odds anyways. I think that's better than having a huge question mark over your head wondering what your chances are. If you are in a low female area it means that you will likely have to sell yourself more to get a date (more on what selling yourself is and how to do it later).

As far as demographics go, I am just asking you to be aware of them and their influence on your chances. This does not mean that you can't find a woman if you live in a state with more men than women, of course you can! It just helps to be aware of your situation and how much effort might be needed to sway the odds of getting the girl. Speaking of playing the odds, another bit of information for you to think over is that the better-looking a woman is, the more likely she is to be single. Yes, I know that would seem to not make sense. Keeping demographic factors in mind, the reason a very attractive girl can still be single even in a highly male populated area is simple to understand. Aside from other factors like she just broke up with her boyfriend, is new in town, or other little things like that, attractive girls don't get asked out that much because guys find them intimidating! It boils down to understanding human nature and that most guys are too shy, too afraid of rejection, too scared, and too unsure of what to do and say to approach a very attractive woman. Other men also assume that because a woman is so attractive that she must be high maintenance or at least have a boyfriend, and as a result, those very attractive ladies don't get hit up on by other men as much as you would think. This means even if you think you're a fat and ugly guy, you still have a good to fair chance of getting an incredible physically attractive girl! Remember it is human nature to want to be loved and to be with others, and if she is not getting love and attention from other men (for all the reasons and more that I listed already), then you will do just fine.

A little known fact about women is that far more often than not, when you approach them, they are nervous too! They are often concerned about what they should say and what they should do in response to you. They get nervous if they think you are cute in any way. They also get nervous if you say something they like because once they are interested their anxiety starts going up. Women have the advantage of looking more at ease because you are typically the one going to them and having to introduce yourself. Make no mistake about it however: despite how they look, they are nervous too.

Now let's talk about *motivation* as a key issue with the faulty mind. You must have motivation in order to get out there into the world and date. As human beings, one thing that undermines our motivations is our own negative self-talk. We humans are incredibly hard on ourselves, beating ourselves up with thoughts like *I should have done this* or *Why didn't I do that?* We constantly think about and develop patterns of behavior and thoughts that can and often do make us miserable. Everyone beats himself or herself up with negative self-talk at some point in life. It is basic psychology. This is useful to you because it means that now you know that everyone does it, including women. It also means you can stop believing in your negative self-talk with thoughts like *She wouldn't be interested in me* or *I don't have anything to offer her.*

A thought is just a thought and a feeling is just a feeling. Both your thoughts and feelings can and often do change. If you think you're a comic book superhero and can fly, does it mean you're going to fly? Probably not. If you feel you can fly, will you? Probably not. So why not just recognize your negative thoughts as negative thoughts and let them go? Just move on and do what you want. The mind thinks up all kinds of weird stuff. That is part of its job. When you're facing the possibility of rejection your mind is naturally going to start thinking up negative thoughts to keep you from getting hurt. It is a lot like a self-defense mechanism. It is up to you to override that mechanism. This means you need to challenge negative thoughts and think of the positives. For example, if you think *She wouldn't be interested in me,* ask yourself what it is about you that she might be interested in. *She would be interested in me because . . .* It is simple, but it does take time and practice because what you are basically doing is retraining your brain how to think. If you don't do this kind of thinking daily, you are likely to have low self-esteem and a negative outlook on the world in general. Positive thoughts will help motivate you and are a major component to getting and keeping your motivation.

Motivation is a key element to dealing with the faulty mind. If you don't have motivation, then all the facts and know-how in all the dating books ever written will not do you any good. To get your motivation up, to use this book and be successful, you are going to have to ask yourself and answer to yourself some key questions that hopefully will help motivate you to use this book not just read it. You need to ask yourself, *What is it that I really want?,* and *What is it that I don't want?* Let's say you want to date and you don't want to get rejected. You need ask yourself how badly you really want to date? Then ask what you are willing to do to get a date? Ask yourself, *What am I doing to get what I want now in my life? How is that working for me?* With your responses in mind, in order *to make the most out of this book you have to be willing to do the assignments* to become a successful dater. A wise

12

proverb that applies here is "Change for the better requires effort; change for the worse requires none". In other words, you have to work to get what you want! Completing the assignments in this book will tell you what is truly useful for you as an individual. Finally, after utilizing this book, you will formulate your own style of interactions with members of the opposite sex to meet your needs and be a successful dater.

Another bit of potentially motivational information for you to think about is that women, like guys, talk about sex, generally want sex, and joke about sex and guys every bit as much as men do! What this should tell you is that women are not generally as hard to get as you might think. What creates the problem is getting past the fears women have of dating the wrong guy or the wrong kind of guy. Additionally they might set up defensive walls to avoid feeling bad about themselves or looking like a slut in front of their friends in the club. Let us move on to the next chapter on attitudes.

CHAPTER 3

How to Have and Show the Right Attitude

"By three methods we may learn wisdom: first, by reflection,
which is noblest; second, by imitation, which is easiest; and third,
by experience, which is the most bitter."
~ Confucius

Self-Acceptance

This chapter highlights the three methods that you may learn
from. Reflection is needed to gain self-acceptance. Imitation
is needed in the form of various body languages to attract a
woman. Last but not least, experience is needed to learn from
mistakes. Naturally, we want to maximize learning from past
mistakes and minimize future mistakes. One of the ways you can
minimize future mistakes is to reflect on your attitude.

Attitude didn't make it into the faulty mind chapter because it
is something that we show others and others can often see within
us. Every man knows what he wants when he sees it, particularly
when it's a sexy girl. Some men lack the confidence and guts
to use that "I want you" attitude that they have inside, because
they are just too shy or afraid of rejection to express it. Think of
it like this, you know you look at hot women all the time, talk
about them with your friends, and fantasize about being with

them. That's natural. You're a guy and that's what guys do. The problem is you hold those feelings in and never approach the girl, or if you do your attitude projects an image of shyness. Shyness can be cute but being shy is almost never going to get you the girl, much less keep her! Women want a man, and that means being strong, honest, and having a *take-charge attitude.* It is that very same shyness that blocks you from truly accepting yourself and showing the right attitude with women. Start developing some self-acceptance by being honest with yourself. Stop making excuses for not approaching women or being less than truthful about why you want to talk to them, and above all don't apologize to them or to whoever you pray to for wanting a woman in any way. You're human and humans have needs and desires. Admit to and accept your feelings. Feelings may change but in the moment that you first feel an attraction, of desire, it is that feeling you should focus and act on when meeting someone. Your feelings are there for a reason. From there, your self-accepting attitude will come and show naturally. As you do this, you will naturally feel more okay with who you are and develop more confidence and more positive thoughts that will show in your attitude.

Someone with a positive attitude is always a welcomed person into the life of someone who is going to be worth your time. Now, to be clear, you need to create a balance. If your attitude is too positive or you're too confident, you can come off as annoying or too cocky and that is a turn off for the vast majority of women. There is a difference between confident and arrogant and we will cover that topic in another section of this book. For now, just recognize that the arrogant man does sometimes get the girl but rarely does he keep her. The primary reason for this is that no lady wants to be in a relationship with someone that they feel they can't measure up to. An arrogant man takes confidence to the next level, overcompensating for his insecurities, and he is unwilling to admit them to others, sometimes even to himself. Often arrogant men tear women down rather than build them up to make themselves feel better. That is basically what a bully does, not a man.

Up on Display

Along with self-acceptance leading to people picking up on your confidence and attitude, how do we express our strength, honesty, and take-charge attitude? How can we put ourselves up on display for the world to see? It is pretty simple, and you do it every time you're around your friends.

Think of how you are when you're speaking to your best friend, or go talk to him or her after reading this. Notice your tone of voice and your rate of speech and how relaxed you are speaking with your friend who knows you so well and cares about you, and who you trust. This is how you should be when meeting a total stranger! The word *generalized* in psychology basically means to take a learned set of skills and apply them to new and different situations in life. What you need to do is learn to generalize how you are with a good friend to how you are with women. I am not saying you should tell them everything about yourself right away like you might do with friends. What I am saying is to be as warm and friendly and relaxed around them as you would be around one of your best friends. Think about it like this: when you are with a good friend I bet you are yourself (this takes strength), honest about what you want, what you think, and how you feel. You probably have that "Let's go do this . . ." take-charge attitude naturally and ask a friend to go to a movie with you or play pool or whatever.

To put yourself up on display means not only having the right attitude but also using your body language to develop the right attitude. The mind in part reacts to the physical sensations of the body. If you walk, talk, sit, and feel comfortable as you are with your friends, then you're going to be more comfortable in any place or any situation including with members of the opposite sex! In a very real and effective manner, this is what people mean by "Be yourself." Only most people don't know what that really means, and how to act on it. Often because you are not used to being yourself with people other than friends, it can feel awkward. That's okay. It takes time and practice, but once you act and feel the way you do with your close friends, around girls your odds of being a successful dater go up.

Remember that people suffer and everyone likes to have a positive, friendly person in his or her life. Not only are you less likely to get rejected, but you will also likely find yourself being invited out by friends and other people more often. The more you're out, the better your chances of finding a date.

What follows are more tips on how to make others feel comfortable around you and to actually make yourself feel that way too.

Facial Expressions

Your face can tell another person how you are feeling. A frown means someone is upset or sad, a straight unemotional face could mean many things like the person is thinking or just good at hiding what he thinks or feels. A smile naturally means the person is happy, right? Well, guess what. One of your best weapons is your smile. Yup, you got it, your smile. No, I don't mean that half-ass, mouth-shut smile that you give out to people you barely know on the street. I mean a full-teeth showing, big "I love you" smile.

The smile is a simple and devastating weapon to use on someone. Why? Psychologically, from the time we were born our parents and relatives smiled at us, played with us, and smiled because they love us so much. What does this teach people, even you? It teaches us that a smile is associated with personal warmth, or love if you like, with trust, with security, and it makes you seem like a fun person. It's like that for nearly everybody. Go look in a mirror and practice your best smile. You want a smile that shows at least some of your teeth and is even with your face, meaning don't give one of those half-hearted smiles that come from only half of your face. Smile fully with your best smile. After all, you like it when some girl smiles at you so it makes sense women like this too. It's not really necessary to go out and buy a book on how to read facial expressions in order to figure out how you should react to others or to read what their thinking or feeling. Normally we learn this kind of thing naturally and may forget over time, hence this section of the book. If you want to go buy a book on this subject for more information, it can't hurt. Most books on this topic are about the same. Just be sure to pick one up with lots of pictures.

Body Language

Your posture like your face sends a message too—before you even speak to the person you are interested in. It can say, "Hey I'm a lazy, kick-back/depressing kind of guy with my shoulders hunched over." Or it can say, "Wow, I'm really not interested in what you have to say." Worse still, your body language can say, "I lack confidence in myself" or "I'm not really looking to date anyone." In short, your body language can say a whole lot. Think of your favorite movie star that you would like to be. Personally, mine's James Bond who gets the attention of the hottest girl from across the room as he slowly but confidently makes his approach.

The biker or gangster strolls are modern-day replicas of this confident stroll designed to convey a message of power and identification. Now to be clear, you don't need to be anything other than yourself to get what you want. You don't need to come off as an asshole or a jerk. You can still have your normal attitude and convey a message of confidence to others, while still displaying a sense of humor and a friendly smile.

What I am saying is that in order to project and actually have confidence in yourself you need to act like it! You can be all kinds of confident inside, but it is how you act and what you do that lets other people see it. It's like playing an instrument—practice makes perfect. The more you project confidence, the more often you will develop and have it naturally and at all times, and most importantly, others will be able to tell. In other words, the more you show it, the more natural it will be.

Here is a list of what to do and why you should do it to get that confidence.

1) Stand up straight with your shoulders back and suck in that gut even if you don't have one. Why? There is a great deal of research that show that for both sexes, sticking your chest out, standing tall, and displaying your physical attributes are clear indications to others that you are confident in yourself and most importantly looking to attract someone. What people see is a strong, confident guy. This stance even while walking should remind you of those military movies when the drill sergeant yells at the new recruits to "stand tall, suck in that gut, and stick that chest out, Private!"

2) The walk as I mentioned sends a message about you as a person. I certainly can't tell you how to walk. What I can tell you is that your walk should match up with who you are. If you really think of yourself as a gangster, like that life, and have that mentality, then use that gangster stroll. If you are a biker then use that straight-up, no bullshit, stomping power walk. If you're a cowboy then by all means walk bowlegged. However, if you're a cowboy and dress like it, you would look pretty damn stupid walking like a gangster or even just walking normally (it will show you have never been on a horse). People and especially women can tell when you're full of shit nine out of ten times. Never underestimate your person of interest. It's just like underestimating your enemy. You will get shot down in flames. Instead, check out how you stand and move when walking in a full-length mirror. Determine for yourself if you're conveying the right message in your walk. The best way to do this is to compare your walking style with that of others that you know or can observe who have great success with women and match your own style, or add in a bit of smoothness into yours. Make your walk natural to who you are. On a special note try to avoid the pigeon toe stance where your toes are facing one another. That, my friend, is just an awkward stance and can produce an odd

walk. I suggest getting a modeling book or looking at the stances of male models in magazine and newspaper ads. The reason for this is you can get a very good idea of what stances or poses project confidence and make you look more confident. It beats standing around with your hands in your pockets, looking shy. Science tells us that body language makes up ninety percent of our communication with others. In other words body language is important. Work on it!

The Learning Curve

Putting yourself on display properly takes time. It is very hard to learn to be comfortable in a strange social setting, particularly if your friends are not around. Most people, if not all people, disguise themselves and act one way at home, one way at work, and one way when parents are around. It is not so much that people who act differently from one situation to the next are pretending or masking their true selves. What simply happens in life is we are taught how to behave (typically) by parents in social settings. That means being quiet and not your more relaxed self. As you become more relaxed around others you are likely to make mistakes—not every word out of your mouth will be what someone wants to hear. Some will think the way you sit or walk or the tone of your voice is not really what they want in a guy. Sometimes in life you will even say the wrong thing and turn a woman off. Naturally this book will eliminate many if not most of those mistakes, but let's be honest. No human being ever says or does the right thing at the right time 100 percent of the time. Mistakes are not a bad thing and I encourage you to look at mistakes as learning opportunities.

Here is the brutal truth and something you're not likely to get in any class or self-help book: the truth about mistakes. You are going to make mistakes. That's right, you are going to get all this information and practice, get laid, go out on dates, fall in love and have relationships, and you're still going to make mistakes here and there. That, my friend is life. Only by trail and error can you discover what works best for you.

So why do we make mistakes? The answer is quite simply that "practice makes perfect," and this is why you have your homework assignments. Remember that if you let the little "mistakes" or the occasional complete screw-up keep you down, you will get nowhere in life or with anyone. Learn from your mistakes and grow from them. The odds are that if you're reading this that you don't have that much experience with different kinds of women and in dating. Will you get what you're after the first time out? Yes, you can! Will you get it the fifth time out? Possible, but maybe not. There are only three things you have to remember when things go wrong.

1) Learn from your mistakes! Think about what was said, how you felt, what they said, and what you can do better next time.
2) Remember it's a numbers game. You're banking on your skills, but even the sexiest man on earth is going to get turned down every once in a while by some lady with a boyfriend or problems of her own.
3) Do not, and I repeat, do not let yourself feel bad about it. If you start thinking in circles about how you screwed up without recognizing other possibilities and what you did right, you will lower your confidence and self-esteem and put yourself back at square one. It is just one mistake. There are plenty of other women in the world. This is why a philosophy of life such as Buddhism is so important.

"One who is afraid to examine his past mistakes cannot see the future" is a saying that nicely explains why it is critical to learn from past mistakes. Another one by the poet and philosopher George Santayana states, "Those who cannot remember the past are condemned to repeat it." Bottom line, no matter how you look at it, mistakes are valuable learning tools that must be learned from if you ever hope to improve.

There are people out there, who think of themselves as real players, social chameleons that can blend in with just about any crowd. Such people might tell you if you're going to be a player, you got to act and dress the part. You want to date a cowgirl, dress like a cowboy. You want to be a pimp, dress like a pimp. You want to date a biker chick, dress like a biker and buy a hog (motorcycle). You want to date some pretty-girl cheerleader, join a sport or lie and say you are in a sport, and dress like a jock. These kinds of tricks are far less effective than you might think. It sounds good but what you will find is:

A) You will be spending a whole lot of time and money on your wardrobe.
B) Women will probably see right past your bullshit.
C) Even if they don't see past your smoke screen right away, they will at some point, perhaps even before you have gotten what you wanted.
D) This tactic requires a whole lot of effort and can and often does involve lying about yourself and who you are both verbally and visually. Typically that will kill any chance at a relationship.

Why bother? Trust me on this: you don't need to resort to those kinds of tricks to get a woman. Acting and dressing the part of what you think a woman wants does not give you the ability and understanding of what women want in a man. Women want confidence, humor, trust, and friendliness. Save yourself the effort of having to learn what I am telling you here the hard way. Those are the kind of tactics that are for the dirty, sleazy person who is so obsessed with getting what he wants and is of such low character and self-esteem that he is willing to toss out his morals and pieces of his personality just on the *possibility* of getting into bed with someone who only dates jocks, bikers, gangsters, gangster wannabes, etc. Not only is this sad, but if a girl is that superficial then believe me she is so not worth your time, or your cash, much less that kind of effort.

How to Get Rejected

The following story a perfect and personal example of the numbers game, how we learn by experience, and example of being rejected at no fault of your own. To be honest, at this time in my life I had *slept with* more than actually *dated* very hot girls, and by *hot* you should be thinking models. I didn't feel the need to commit to one girl until I started dating this one girl for three months. She was hot, and I mean Victoria's Secret catalog hot. Not only was she hot, but more importantly in terms of having a relationship with her she was perfect. Yes, I mean *perfect*. She laughed at all my jokes. She was a great conversationalist, she was just what I wanted in the bedroom, she cooked, and she cleaned and picked small fights with me just for fun and makeup sex. The problem was, as perfect as she was, I just didn't have any feelings of love for her. *Lust* yes, *love* no. This drove me nuts for the last month of our dating relationship. As an introspective person and a psychology major at the time, I analyzed myself to no end thinking the fault must be with me. Eventually, I came to realize that sometimes no matter how great the person is, the other person might just not be emotionally attracted to you and needs to move on. Some people might call emotional attraction *chemistry,* or *picking up on someone else's vibe, aura,* or *spiritual energy,* or *spark.* This is true, and I'm not some New Age hippy, but think about it for yourself.

I bet you can recall a time or place that you were walking down the street or at some party and you saw or even met someone that for no real reason you just didn't like or the person gave you the creeps. This is what I am talking about. I and about every other guy in school were attracted to this girl I was dating physically, but for me the bus stopped there. So keep in mind that that it is a numbers game and the reason she might say *no* to you is she's just inexplicably not *(at no fault of yours or hers)* attracted to you. That's fine, that's life, move on. Other than this being the case and out of your control, the whole text is geared to not getting rejected.

I wanted to include here a helpful tactic that is a big reason for success with women and particularly helpful in *not* getting rejected. In psychology this technique is referred to as *guided imagery*. I put it here because if you don't do this, putting yourself on display can be more difficult and you are more likely to get rejected.

Guided imagery is a psychology technique developed, believe it or not, via the meditation practices from the orient. When most guys think about going up to a girl we think about what we are going to say and how she will respond in advance. It's normal for us to think a few moves ahead, but you should never picture yourself going up to someone and hitting it off right away with someone, while you say all the right things as if you were a ghost looking at or out of your own body and watching a play or a movie. Doing this sets you up for failure because you're outside your body and looking at a *display case* of how you hope it will go and how you hope you will feel. When you're in the moment talking to a lady, you are in your body not outside it! The result is often feelings of nervousness and feeling improperly prepared. This could greatly undermine your efforts. What you should do is put yourself in your body and imagine what's going to happen though your own eyes. Think of this as a first-person point-of-view mode in one of those popular video games. How are you going to feel, what sounds are around you? What are you going to say and how will you say it? More importantly, how will she respond? Using this kind of mentally guided imagery is one very big reason for success with women because before anything even happens you are planning out your moves just like in chess. And as any good philosopher will tell you, if you imagine success you will likely get it. It's a concept called a self-fulfilling prophecy. You get the results you expect.

Learning from Our Past Again

By this time you have likely made some mistakes out in the dating world on your own before you ever started reading this book. Think back. What can you learn from them? Probably one big thing you felt at some point was a great deal of anxiety when approaching someone you were interested in but did not know. I want you to think back to a time when you felt good about yourself. Perhaps it was one of those times that you did get laid or fixed up a car or bought a new car. Perhaps it was when you won a race or it was a competition of some kind, or even something as simple as receiving good feedback from one of your teachers (you're so smart, you did a good job, etc . . .). Along with being warm and friendly as if you were going to talk to one of your best friends, this is want you want to feel inside when you approach someone. So once you have made up your mind to introduce yourself to someone, think of that very best moment in your life that you felt really good about yourself, hold on to that feeling, and go for it. This will build up your confidence and the other person, as well as the people around her, will pick up on your confidence too. Eventually, you will feel this way the majority of the time without having to use this little trick. This technique works because you cannot feel two incompatible emotions at the same time. For instance, you cannot be both scared and relaxed at the same time. You will be more relaxed while others check you out when you're up on display.

Homework Assignment 0

Self-esteem is a critical factor in dating. I call this "Homework Assignment 0" because you don't have to do a thing outside your home to complete it. As an exercise in building your self-esteem, complete the requirements of each bullet point.

- Write down at least five of your strengths, such as persistence, courage, friendliness, and creativity.
- Write down at least five things you admire about yourself, such as the way you have raised your children, your good relationship with your brother, or your spirituality.

- Write down the five greatest achievements in your life so far, like recovering from a serious illness, graduating from high school, or learning to use a computer.

Homework Assignment 1

Go to a place of your choosing and ask out (using the skills and information you have learned so far) ten people and keep track of how many of them said *yes*. You can ask out ten people in one place like a bar or spread them out and ask a few here and there (at a bar, grocery story, the DMV, etc.). A recent study claimed that even the most unattractive guy could get one out of every ten girls to go out on a date. There was even a television spoof of this where on one show a guy asked for sex from ten real-world (meaning they were not actors) women and one of them said *yes*. However she was quite unattractive. Remember you are asking for a date and not sex, at least not yet, one thing at a time.

The point of this exercise is to determine your current level of functioning. During each attempt you should note what difficulty you are having talking to women. It will help you and tell you what it is you most need to improve on. Additionally, this will provide you with a real tangible gauge on how well your dating skills are currently, and how much they have improved after reading this book. Yes, this does mean you will be doing this assignment again toward the end of this book.

I included this homework assignment here and not at the very start of this book because I figured there was no point in making your life harder than it has to be. This way you get some information on how to take and learn from your mistakes. It is important to look at mistakes as a learning process and this assignment as an *experiment* because if you allow yourself to get caught up in your own feelings of joy (if she says *yes)* or sadness (if you get rejected), then you will miss out on the critical information that you need to improve. You will not know exactly what you did to get the date or what you may have done to get rejected because you were too busy focusing on the outcome and not *the process*.

This is my way of telling you that for this assignment, relax. Put your thinking cap on and take your emotions out of it as best you can. Hope for the best but don't worry even if all ten women reject you. This is a learning process and you are just starting to learn.

At this point I recommend you re-read from the start of this book up to this point and take at least a week to digest the material and try it out. After that you can continue reading chapter 4.

CHAPTER 4

Cognitive Appraisals and You, Part 2

"Not to alter one's faults is to be faulty indeed."
~ Confucius

The Faulty Mind Revisited

We are coming back to this subject because at this point we have worked on faulty thinking and attitudes about women and yourself. We have even touched on how to build up your confidence. With this done, we return to the subject to reinforce what you have learned so far.

The faulty mind likes to think very negative thoughts, such as *I can't* . . . or *She won't* . . . It is critical beyond all words that you start to recognize or catch your mind when you have those negative thoughts that keep you from doing what you want. In the case of dating, those thoughts often keep you from introducing yourself to a girl and asking her out on a date. To combat these negative thoughts you have to do three things. First be aware of when you have them. Second, challenge them. Third, don't believe them.

Here is an example of what I mean. Let's say you're at a party and you spot a girl you want to get to know. The thought pops up in your head that you can't go talk to her and is followed by a feeling of anxiety/nervousness. First recognize the thought and feeling. You might have the thought that you don't like that feeling. Second, challenge the thought *I can't go talk to her*. The truth is you can, but your anxiety/nervousness is so unpleasant for you that you *feel* that you can't go talk to her. The truth is you can!

A thought is just a thought and a feeling is just a feeling. You can sit around thinking you're Superman all day long, but that doesn't mean you're going to fly. You can tell yourself over and over that you *can't talk* to some girl, but you always can. You have a choice! Do not let your faulty thoughts keep you from getting what you want. Even the thought "*She wouldn't like me*" is garbage. You don't know that. You can't know that. For all you know, you could remind her of her last boyfriend that she loved but who left her because he had to move away. Even if you feel anxious in the moment, feelings change and as you do, go up and talk to her, there is a good chance you won't feel that way when she is laughing and smiling at your jokes and funny stories.

Typically those kinds of anxiety-provoking thoughts come from putting women on mental pedestals. Putting a woman on a pedestal is the single greatest mistake you can make. I am not saying to treat women like dirt. What I am saying is *do not think that they are any better or worse than you are*. "Never confuse the extent of one's fame with the extent of one's character" is another proverb that fits in well here. In other words, no matter how popular or beautiful a girl is, she is just a person, same as you and me. Women don't deserve your love or respect any more than anyone else does until they earn it! Think of it this way: has this person you're interested, this person you just met or have yet to even speak to, earned the right to be put up on a pedestal by you? No way. And if by virtue of her looks alone you think she has, before you have even spoken to her you are way too easily impressed. If you're that easily impressed, then getting your respect or admiration is about as valuable as a rusty crutch that's missing a screw. In other words, you're likely to fall on your butt and break something. What I am getting at is if you fall "in love" right away and think someone is better than you or too good for you, then that person is not going to respect you. People must earn your respect.

The best way to get respect is to earn it. If you truly want to impress others, you are going to have to do something with your time other than chasing after women. "Never seek happiness outside yourself" is an old saying. If you try to find respect and happiness outside yourself, you are likely to end up a hollow shell of what you could have been. On the other hand, people who tell you that if you want to find someone you should stop looking, are lucky or idealistic fools. "Seek and you shall find." What people really mean to say is *stop being so needy!* That means stop needing the love and attention of others so much and start being comfortable with who you are. It also means that you just need to be yourself. This means your value as a person is not based off who you are with. This means you need balance in your life as a single person.

All you need to do to achieve this is find something fun to do away from women! If you're constantly around members of the opposite sex, guess what? Every once in a while, if not constantly, you are going to be thinking about them and not so much on what you should be doing. The opposite sex can be a great distraction, but if you focus on them too much they become an obsession. We may be envious of that guy we know who has women at his beck and call. That womanizer that so many men look up to typically does not have a lot going for him in life. He spends all his time trying to get, make, keep happy, and get laid by women. This leaves little room for anything else. So get out there in the world and do something you enjoy that's rated PG-13 so you can tell your grandkids about it one day.

Doing something for yourself actually makes you a more interesting person. No one cares about how you sat on your butt all day long, and in all honesty no one cares how much or what you drank last night. The stories of how many women you slept with get old and repetitive and do not say much about your character. Instead, go out, enjoy your life, and do things you have always wanted to do. Go camping, climb Everest, skydive, hang glide, travel, read a good book, join a club, or take up a sport, whatever it is that you enjoy. In the end, because you have other things to worry about and enjoy in life (other than women), you will have part of that "I don't need you but you need me" attitude that women respond to, and that we will talk about more in later chapters.

A special word on video games as something to do away from women. Games are really popular in today's society, but it is easy to get lost in them. You don't want to end up a forty-year-old video game addict that's never had any real fun with women outside video games. Seriously, gaming is like an addiction so watch how much you play. If you can do it, try to give it up completely and only play if the girl you end up with wants to play. Another way to look at it is that it is harder to keep a girlfriend when you're more interested in video games than her.

Giving Them What They Think They Want

People always want what they can't have. Boys and girls alike are always striving for what is just beyond their reach. It's human nature. Only after we wise up are we happy for what we do have in our lives. Some people call this personal growth, others call it enlightenment. It's something that many hope for as they get older. So what key thing can you do to capture someone's interest? Aside from having a hobby, or a body like a Greek statue if she is superficial, that consists of one word, one thought, one attitude. The best thing you can say to a woman is simply the word *no*. That's it. Women, especially really beautiful women, are used to having men cave in and bend over backward to their will, giving them just what they want. By saying *no* to her you're telling her that she is not the boss. I tried like crazy to find this quote or something like it online but could not, so I admit here that it is not mine but there is a saying I want to share with you. "The man who does best with women can do without them." Basically it means you have to have the attitude that they need you and not the other way around!

By saying *no* you're telling her, "You're not going to walk all over me," and most of all you're telling her she cannot control you. In short, you become a challenge, something attainable but just beyond her reach. This is a really hard thing to do because the faulty mind might tell you that you should try to make her happy. In reality, it is not your responsibility to try to make anyone happy, much less all of the time. So yes, it sucks, you will feel bad and mentally torture yourself over saying *no,* but try to remember *you can't make anyone happy all of the time.*

Ignore those temporary feelings of guilt or desire and suck it up. It's hard to do but when you do, you will find that your sense of confidence will go up, you will like yourself more, and she will respect you in the long run. Like the football player, you have to recognize that a play could cost you a few yards, but the real focus is on making the touchdown. Another way to think about it is, like in war, this is called *collateral damage.* Glance at what you have to lose but focus on what you want to win. It's something you should say to yourself before you start dating and sometime shortly after you start dating.

Being Courageous

The faulty mind wants you to give into fear. Feeling brave is part of what helps get guys to introduce themselves to women. Sadly, as you can see at bars and parties, a lot of men rely on liquid courage (alcohol). This might seems strange and you might think that one thing has nothing to do with the other, but if you are brave and courageous in other things, approaching women will be less frightening for you. The thing is, you can't do brave and courageous things that don't make you fearful. You have to challenge yourself to overcome those things that actually do make you afraid. For instance, if you're not afraid of heights, climbing a mountain and standing on its top won't help you because you never had that fear. Overcoming your actual fears will leave you with a sense of accomplishment, pride, confidence, personal power, and a sense of manly strength that you will carry around with you always. Challenging yourself to overcome your fears will help you have that natural confidence you're looking for. Don't believe me? Just look at most of the men in the armed forces and how confident they are. They have to challenge and overcome many obstacles and the vast majority of them do have great confidence.

A Few Extra Tips

When the mind is faulty it produces feelings both emotionally and physically. You must master your mind to feel more courageous and to learn how to relax a bit. It is a lot harder to be courageous when your feeling of anxiety is so high you can hardly move. To become more courageous just try smiling. It is a proven fact that when you smile you release a small amount of "happy" chemicals directly to your brain. It only helps a little but some help is better than none. If smiling can help you relax and be more courageous even by as little as 1 percent it will help to get the ball rolling. A smile may make the difference in helping you get the courage to go meet the girl and getting the date or not even trying or being rejected by her.

Visualized breathing: Taking deep breaths is a tried and true method in therapy. First notice your body and the feeling you don't like and give it a color and see it in your mind's eye. Now think of your favorite color. Now imagine that there are tiny particles in the air that if you look real close, like the light shining through a window, you can see the reflection of those particles in the air. Take deep or normal breaths and notice the air fill your lungs as if it could almost touch your belly when you breathe it in. Now imagine breathing in that good reflective color and imagine it scrubbing gently away bit by little bit with every breath. Some of that bad color in your body goes out your mouth.

Transfer of energy: We know that energy can transfer. It is a scientific fact. For example, we can transfer heat energy from one object to another. Notice your breath and how it circulates in the body. Feel the feeling you want to get rid of. Now imagine a color to that feeling/energy and use the energy you normally have in your gut when you breathe to push the undesired colored energy out through your arms or feet and into the ground or some object you are touching.

Visualized breathing and transfer of energy techniques work because you are forcing the electro-chemical signals in the brain to the imaginative centers of the brain. Basically, you're changing the flow of electricity in your head in such a way that there is not enough electrical power for you to feel as anxious when you are doing this technique. In short, you can't feel anxious when you're focused on something other than your anxiety.

CHAPTER 5

What to Say and How to Say It

"It's not what you say; it's how you say it."
~ Unknown

Conveying Warmth

This is perhaps the most critical chapter of the book. Being nice and friendly seems easy, but there is an art to it. A college friend of named Steve who attends church every week is loved and adored by scores of women, and why is that? Well, first off, he doesn't come off as some sex-crazed animal. He approaches them with all the friendliness, kindness, warmth, and fun that he can. It doesn't matter if she is a pretty girl, a biker girl, or any other type of girl. They all love him. I was suspicious of this—just because they all seemed to think he was the greatest guy didn't mean they would go out with him. Steve was only about five feet, four inches tall, and he was in good shape but a bit thick in the middle and he had glasses. It's safe to say he would be considered average in most people's books. After asking ten girls (who I knew were single) if they would be interested in giving him a shot (meaning going out on one date) seven of them said *yes!* I was stunned! He had not even been trying, and seven great-looking college cuties would have said yes if he had ever had the nerve to ask them out. Sadly,

Steve's self-esteem when it came to dating was so low that he never did ask any of them out for fear of rejection. Even when I told him they would say *yes!*

The point is having a friendly attitude works. It's human nature to want to interact with people. Even hermits that live alone in the mountains want the occasional interaction with someone, some of the time. Every person, no matter how cold or distant they may seem, wants to feel liked, loved, respected, appreciated, and cared for. A lot of nice guys are friends with girls; this is not what I am talking about (however this is covered in another chapter). What I am talking about is having a friendly attitude toward women.

For now, try setting aside your desire for sex and, if nothing else, be friendly with her—not all hot and heavy and eager to get into her pants. You may find that you like her more as a friend than you would as a lover. Better still, perhaps you will start off as friends and end up lifelong lovers.

Your Tone of Voice and the Message It Conveys

If you approach with warmth and friendliness, it's a pretty safe way to meet someone at no cost to you, and as an added benefit, you can subtly scope her out to explore her character if you're after a relationship. If, however, you go up to her nervous or unsure, you may very well convey in the tone of your voice "fear," and that is going to tell her you're a weak-willed kind of guy. Worse still, you might try to approach her, but because of your unwillingness to learn from your past mistakes you're going to act like such an idiot that she will end up rejecting you. *Your own evil version of a self-fulfilling prophecy.* "People become what they expect themselves to become," Mahatma Gandhi said. In other words, you get the results you expect.

No matter how slick and clever you are, if you use a tone of voice that sounds fearful or creepy the other person is going to become fearful or creeped out by you. Your next homework assignment will teach you how to watch your tone of voice.

Homework Assignment 2

If you couldn't tell from the story of my friend Steve, this is critical homework. If you blow off the other homework assignments, don't blow this one off! Your tone of voice is the most critical aspect of how a woman is going to perceive you. To work on your tone, you must practice the alphabet or some movie line that you like in a mean, aggressive voice once and then in your warmest and friendliest voice next. You will need to practice once a day for five minutes each day for a week or more if you feel you need it. I prefer the alphabet because that way you say every letter using a friendly tone and I think this will come out in your speech more. Then pretend as if you are talking to your favorite pet or childhood friend in that warm and friendly voice for five minutes. Don't baby-talk—obviously that won't work with women . . . unless there is a baby around and you're talking to the baby. Completing this homework will help you to convey a sense of warmth, comfort, and friendliness to people you talk to. This is absolutely critical because no matter what you say, your tone of voice and body posture convey most of your message. It's that old saying, "It's not what you say; it's how you say it."

When you have the correct tone of voice, people are more likely to instantly bond with you and this creates the added benefit of helping you to *put yourself in a mentally relaxed state of mind when speaking to someone.* The result is you're perceived more positively by others, and you will have more confidence and reduced anxiety when speaking to people.

A fun little option in this homework assignment is to get a voice recorder and practice the alphabet with different tones of voice. Alternatively, or once you are done with saying the alphabet, think of what you what you want to say to some really attractive girl and play it back. Listen for any um's, ah's, and so's in your rate of speech and for the tone of voice you have when talking. Listen to see if you can't hear some fear, some hesitation, some doubt. Then try it again playing with the pitch of your voice and working to eliminate the fear, hesitation, and doubt.

Doing this is a great way to get feedback on not only your tone of voice but also the message it might be sending others. If you do this often enough, you can develop not only a friendly tone but also a sexy tone of voice that women will respond to. If you don't know what your sexy tone should sound like, pick a movie with your favorite actor and try to copy the way he uses his smooth movie lines. From there it is up to you to use that same tone or smoothness in your conversations in life.

Once you are done training yourself to vary your tone of voice, try it out with friends and family members. Practice using a soft sad tone, a smooth seductive tone, a fun friendly tone, a seriously important tone, and so on. To get good at using tone you just have to open your ears and listen to the tones of others.

You should at this point take another week off to digest and practice all you have learned up to this point. Yes, chapters 4 and 5 are that critical and worth the practice. You should be taking the time to reread both chapters and do the homework. That's why chapter five is so short!

CHAPTER 6

The Keys to the Kingdom: Communication

"Ultimately the bond of all companionship, whether
in marriage or in friendship, is conversation . . ."
~ Sir Oscar Wilde

How to Be a Conversational Wizard

So at this point we have worked on your cognitive appraisals
and addressed many key issues found within the faulty mind.
You now have an idea of what to say, and more importantly *how* to
say it. In this chapter were going to cover how to assess your target
of interest and how to approach her. Let's say you approach and
speak, she laughs, and/or is flattered by what you say. Now what?

Most often in the course of a conversation the person will say
something that you're interested in or that you know something
about. What colossal mistake do most people make? They jump
in and start talking about their experiences and/or themselves.
Do not do this! Remember that people like to talk and especially
about *themselves*.

Jumping in or taking control of the conversation and making
it about you or about some topic or issue in this way is not

good because you can be seen as a jerk for taking control of the conversation. The other person may want to talk more or may find what you have to say is boring. What will eventually happen is the other person will ask you a question and invite you to talk. When this happens you need to keep your responses short but informative and interesting and then ask/invite them to talk more about that or a related subject. The more you talk, the greater the chance you will say something that she doesn't like, thus lowering your chances of getting what you want.

Learning how to be a conversational wizard can be a very complex chore. It can be difficult because there are so many different personality types in the world, people are so different, and different people converse differently depending on the situation and whom they are talking to. To be a conversational wizard takes a great deal of practice . . . normally. What I am teaching you in this section is how to be an excellent conversationalist in a short amount of time, in a manner that is easy to do and remember. After just a little practice you will be ahead by leaps and bounds in the conversation department in comparison to the vast majority of other people.

One common mistake that most people do is hurrying the conversation. We are so used to fast-paced interaction. The truth is you have about five to seven seconds max before you have to respond to someone. That is plenty of time to look up and think about what the person said. They won't think you're slow; instead people figure you are really thinking about what they said. Even if you're just thinking about what to say next.

The majority of people make the mistake of asking question after question in an effort to keep a conversation going, or, worse, still talk too much because they are nervous.

Here I will give you an example of a common mistake and how to correct it. By applying the information in this section you can easily avoid or correct any such mistakes in any conversation.

The end result of this chapter will arguably be your biggest and best weapon in life and will not only get you the date but all the dates after. For people in relationships this section can improve the communication and quality of your relationship.

Let's start off with the point that I mentioned above: asking too many questions. For the purpose of example, I'll use a very easy and basic one.

You: Hi, I was just wondering what your necklace says. I couldn't make it out from over there.

Her: Oh, well, it says Best Friends Forever.

You: That's cool. Who's your best friend?

Her: Her name's Stacy.

You: That's nice, how long have you two been friends?

Her: Eight years.

You might ask where they met or some other random question, but notice that her responses are short, just responding to what you asked and little else. These questions are referred to in psychology as closed questions. They invite only minimum response and little or no room to start a real conversation. Even if she gave you more information, you would be left having to ask more questions that you don't really care about while trying to figure out how to steer the conversation to something that you want to know, namely more about her and not her friend. You could ask what they were doing when they met, etc . . . , and take the long road to get to what you really want, but there are several bad points to this style of conversation. This kind of conversation leaves you constantly trying to figure out what to say next. Even worse is that in the course of this conversation, should you find yourself asking question after question it makes the conversation feel forced and the person may grow suspicious and think you're creepy and/or weird for wanting to know so much about them.

Even if the person you're talking with was to talk constantly, there would come a point that you may very well be left with what I like to call *dead space*. Others might call it *empty space*. I call it *dead space* because it's that point in the conversation that you began to realize you're in trouble (i.e., dead meat). It's that space in the conversation that is quiet and no one else is talking. Why does this happen? Because no one knows what to say next and the conversation has spun out of control.

So how the heck are you supposed to get to know a person and just what the heck are you supposed to say? The best way to win someone over in a conversation is using a technique that therapists have been using for a long time: active listening. This is a style of conversation that achieves several important goals.

1) It establishes trust.
2) It invites them to tell you more about themselves without feeling forced to respond.
3) It validates their feelings and thoughts making them feel good about you (as if you understand and are connecting with them) and themselves.

Before you know it they are opening up to you and feeling downright comfortable with you. How does this work? Essentially after asking your first question or making your first statement (inviting them to speak), you control the conversation by asking open-ended questions, by paraphrasing and repeating what they said, and if you want adding in a stated question about how they might think or feel. Don't worry—it sounds harder than it is.

Open-ended or Clarifying Questions

Asking an open-ended question is pretty simple and more likely to get the other person to talk more than just asking a question that she can respond to quickly. Essentially this is learning how, when, and what questions to ask. Sticking with our example, let's start the conversation over so you can see the difference in asking an open-ended question.

You: Hi, I was just wondering what your necklace says. I couldn't make it out from over there.

Her: Oh, well, it says Best Friends Forever.

You: Oh, yeah? Tell me more about her (said with slight tilting of the head to convey interest and a question).

Her: Well, her name is Stacy; we met in school eight years ago at a concert, and we just kind of hit it off and have been best friends ever since.

What you did here was invite her to give as much information as she wanted and you got three pieces of information from her all with one question. Her friend's name is Stacy. They met eight years ago, and at a concert. The secret to asking good open-ended questions is to start the sentence off with key words, such as who, what, when, where, and how. Avoid using the word *why* as much as possible as it tends to create a defensive feeling in others. Example: "Why, did you do that?" is likely to provoke a defensive reaction. Asking *why* generally forces a person to produce an internal reason. "What led you to do that?" is less likely to result in someone becoming defensive. It allows for the person to think about what was in the environmental surroundings that produced the action and is much less likely to produce defensiveness.

Well, now what? More questions: "How close are you?" "What was the concert?" "What do you do for work?" "What does Stacy do for work?" "Do you like to go bungee jumping?" How's that for a random, very awkward, and off-topic question? This is not how you want the conversation to go or worse for you to be perceived as a creep. What you do then is mix it up with some summarization/paraphrasing skills.

Summarization/Paraphrasing Skills

All you have to do to break up those endless questions is summarize or paraphrase what the other person just said. It may sound silly, but it works.

What you should do is at some point of your choosing, take what she just said or has said so far and restate it.

You: So you met Stacy at some concert eight years ago and became best friends.

Or

You: So you're very close to her.

Paraphrasing and restating what they just said looks ridiculous in type. Most people are afraid to use this technique because they feel like the other person will pick up on what they are doing and think that they are stupid or that they are not paying attention.

Nothing could be further from the truth. This technique works and if you don't believe it, remember that psychologists and counselors use it all over the world every day, and here is why. When you paraphrase and repeat back what they just said, you are showing them that you are in fact paying attention and hanging on to their every word. Women love this!

You: So you met Stacy at some concert eight years ago and became best friends.

Or

You: So you're very close to her.

Her: Yeah, it was a great concert, but I have not been to one in a long time. Next time they come to town I want to go. I'd go with Stacy, but she just moved away . . .

Or

Her: Yeah, we met at a concert eight years ago; her name is Stacy. I have not been to a concert in a long time. Next time they come to town, I want to go. I'd go with Stacy, but she just moved away . . .

You: Ah, so next time that concert comes to town you want to see them again.

See, it's easy and can produce the same or very similar results regardless of how much or little they say.

Reflection

Reflection is a lot like summarization but you add in a guess as to how the other persons feels or felt in their story. Essentially you are holding up a mirror to the other person and asking her if this is how she feels.

You can even do this by adding a question using the tone of your voice and body language to a statement/summary. Let's return to the same scenario for the sake of keeping things simple.

You: So you met Stacy at some concert eight years ago and became best friends? (Adding a slight pitch to the tone of your voice to make it a questioning statement and/or tilting your head slightly to one side shows interest.)

You will probably also find out more information in the course of your conversation. For instance, you may find out the she was not best friends with Stacy right after the concert but just met her there. They really started their friendship a few weeks later at a mutual friend's party.

Her: Yeah, it was a great concert, but I have not been to one in a long time. Next time they come to town, I want to go. I'd go with Stacy, but she just moved away . . .

Remember, better still is when you reflect back to them a guess at what they might be feeling.

Her: Yeah, it was a great concert, but I have not been to one in a long time. Next time they come to town, I want to go. I'd go with Stacy, but she just moved away . . .

You: So now that your best friend of eight years has moved away, you must be pretty sad.

Her: Well, yeah, I am pretty sad. I just wish she didn't have to go, but her boyfriend wanted to go work in Nevada, and she loves him, so she decided to go with him.

You: You're sad she moved away to be with the guy she loves and left her friends and family behind. Would you ever do that?

This part was important because at this point you have succeeded in getting her to open up to you by establishing an *emotional connection*, by identifying how she feels, and by understanding how *sad* she feels about her friend leaving. In the very last line you restated what she said and added on a stated question that directly relates to her and the conversation you're having. So now you're showing her that you're paying attention to what she has to say and opening up a door that invites her to engage in more conversation that relates directly to her and what you were talking about. If you want the conversation to go another way, you can always take it in another direction because you're in control.

You: You're sad she moved away to be with the guy she loves and left her friends and family behind. I'm sorry to hear that. I know you like to go to concerts, but do you like to play pool at all?

Or

You: So you're sad she moved away to be with the guy she loves and left her friends and family behind. I'm sorry to hear that. I know you like to go to concerts. What other type of music are you into?

I'll ask you to keep in mind again that a conversation can take many directions. Your *goal should not be to find out what you want to know* but rather to *establish a sense of trust,* and having her feeling comfortable around you, because now you know more about her and have this connection that the two of you now share because you know and understand how she feels (at least on this topic). After you have done this, then you can ask what you want to really know, like if taking her to play a game of pool on a date might be something she would enjoy.

Remember again to let the girls do as much of the talking as possible because they might want to change the conversation to something that's more relevant or pressing in their lives and you might just be the person that they open up to, but they can only do this if you let them talk! Plus, if they want to know more about you they will ask about you and/or what you think when they are done.

By doing this you have seemingly established an emotional connection because the two of you and seem to have this real connection now, and boy, she sure does feel comfortable around you my friend! You also are in control, gently steering the conversation. To be completely fair, yes, this sounds pretty manipulative, but honestly this approach requires you to pay attention to what she's saying (people in general tend to like that) and you have probably established a real connection on your part.

After all, if you liked what she had to say or felt similar to what she was saying or expressing, it's possible she got to you just as much as you got to her.

There is admittedly a minor danger in that you could be way off base when guessing at what a woman may be feeling, but it's very fixable.

You: So now that your best friend of eight years has moved away, you must be pretty sad.

Her: No not really. She moved away to be with the guy she loves, and I'm happy for her. I'm more annoyed that she took my favorite blanket with her when she moved out.

Well, now you have learned that's she not so sad at this point in time as she is annoyed about her favorite blanket being taken, along with the additional information that she's happy for her friend and her friend seems to have lived with her before she left.

You: Ah, so you're more annoyed/angry (you can change the word so long as it has about the same meaning) that she took your favorite blanket when she moved out of the place you were staying.

Her: Yeah, you're right I am a bit angry. I mean she knows that's my favorite blanket. I think she took it to remember me by, but it would have been nice if she had asked first.

Since she clarified for you what she really feels, you just have to repeat it back however you like. It's a rigged way of interacting that you can't really lose at!

It's simple to do but important to note that while you're having this conversation you need to use your body language and pick up on hers as well. For instance, if you lean in slightly while talking to one another, this shows interest in the conversation you are having. Leaning back, not so much interest if any at all. Keep eye contact; don't stare at her breasts. One glance doesn't hurt; it shows interest and recognition of her body but not a preoccupation with it because you're really interested in her as a person, hopefully.

So what have we learned?

- Try not to ask stated, short, closed-answer questions.
- Do try to use active listening skills.
- Paraphrase and repeat back to her a part of what she said and that you would like to know more about.

You can do this by paraphrasing and repeating what she says, and by adding a question after repeating what she said using your tone of voice, body language, and by guessing at what she might be feeling. The best key to use is reflection as it establishes a bond. The more you do this the stronger the bond can be.

The best part about active listening is that it works on anyone so, if you don't want to jump out there and try it on someone you're interested in, try using the skills when having conversations with your friends or family. It's extremely, and I do mean extremely, rare for anyone to pick up on what you're doing. If they do, all you have to say is, "Oh, guess I just restated that because I was just thinking about what you said and thought it was interesting . . ." From there you continue your conversation as you normally would because now she knows that you're hanging on to their every word and find them interesting. Who's going to object to that? Combining reflection with clarification and summary skills creates an even smother flow of conversation. I highly recommend that you go online to YouTube and look for a video. Under keyword searches type *active listening* or *reflective listening and counseling.* Something will pop up if you poke around just a little bit that will demonstrate for you how this looks in an actual conversation.

Here is a short list of other effective questions/statements that can lead to more revealing conversations:

- It sounds like . . .
- What I'm kind of hearing in your tone of voice is . . .
- In what way do you feel . . .
- So you feel . . .
- It seems . . .
- I'm sensing . . .
- I'm wondering if . . .
- What I hear you saying is . . .
- What specifically is it . . .
- Could or can you elaborate on that for me?
- How does that apply to what you were talking about awhile back?

Matching

Matching is a simple technique, a subtle, covert kind of communication in psychology. All you have to do is copy or *match* what the other person is saying or doing. This means that you can match someone's rate of speech, hand/or arm gestures, and rate of breathing or verbal expressions. An example of this would be after sex, matching the other person's breathing while cuddling is a great way to enhance the bond of intimacy. You don't want to be too obvious about it so other than the breathing never match her completely and consistently. Match her rate of speech and gestures only a few times during a conversation and only once or twice in full effect (meaning exactly as she does). Some would say this is a manipulative tactic but I look at like imitation is the greatest form of flattery. If you're willing to give this a shot, it just means you like the person enough to try this on some level.

Body Language

Communication as I hope you know by now is more than just verbal; it can also be seen in our body language. There are several clever and simple ways to introduce yourself; if you want to get and keep that girl's attention, you have plenty of options.

It's important that you keep in mind two important things right from the start regardless of your approach. First, if she does not offer to shake your hand when meeting you, *do not* extend your hand to shake hers. The reasons are many. Mostly, you don't want to come off as forceful and be seen as if you're trying to touch her. If she's into you or just has good manners she will likely offer to shake your hand. If this doesn't happen don't let it phase you; it could be she's just shy or nervous.

If she does offer to shake your hand, make sure to shake it firmly. Today many people do half a handshake normally, only grapping the person's fingers. This is not a real handshake—it's a finger shake. An actual handshake should be done palm to palm and a light but firm squeeze. Repeat this information again in your head. It is more important than you think it would be, but a good handshake just like in business tells a lot about the honesty and trust you can place in someone, in this case you.

Some key things to remember in a conversation are to sit and lean in a bit. This shows the person you're talking to that you're interested. Try not to cross your arms or legs, and ideally try not to have a table between the two of you if you can help it. The reasons are simple: if you cross your arms or legs it can be perceived as you are putting up a barrier between the two of you. Just think of the rotten kid who crosses his arms and refuses to leave the store until his mom buys him a toy. The stance is defensive and defiant. You want to be perceived as being open and communicative. This is what you're shooting for.

On the other side of this is the body language of the person you're talking to. If that person is leaning back not making eye contact or sitting on the edge of their seat, he or she is not interested in what you are saying. So it's important to pay attention to this and if necessary change the topic of your conversation until you can see real interest.

Finally, a common mistake many guys make while on first and second dates involves bragging. I include bragging in this section of body language because people who brag tend to convey with their body language lots of confidence. Just keep it in mind that too much confidence can be a bad thing. Think about what's most important for people to know about you *(people,* not just women) and pick three or four things that you are okay with sharing on a date. The reasons for this are several. First and foremost: if you are seen as being a braggart, you can come off as conceited and more into yourself than into her. Not attractive to the ladies. Second, it's possible that if you're bragging is too unbelievable or impressive she might think you're just trying to impress her and are in some way insecure about yourself. This is also unattractive. If your bragging sounds outlandish she may think you are lying to her and to women this makes you less than ideal for dating. Be honest; just pick a few little things to brag about and no more.

The Eye Color Game

I have absolutely no idea where this game came from, but it's been your author's experience that this little game comes up a lot in the course of a conversation. If the girl really likes you and wants to know if you like her, she will suddenly shut her eyes and ask you to tell her what color they are and describe them. Needless to say, when you're having a conversation, take special note of eye color and whether there is more than one color or shade of color in her eyes. You can earn bonus points if you are able to tell her what they remind you of in a slightly romantic way.

CHAPTER 7

Pick-up Facts, Tips, and Tactics

"For just when ideas fail, a word comes in to save the situation."
~ Johann Wolfgang von Goethe

Making the Best of Any Situation

It is basically possible to meet anyone at anytime regardless of the place. For example, it is totally possible to pick up girls on the street, in classes, at coffee shops, at plays, weddings, and funerals, on planes, in movie theaters, and even in front of their moms!

Here are a few things you can say to pick up on the ladies at certain places that might otherwise prove to be a difficult situation for you. As you gain experience and confidence you will be able to make up your own introduction lines.

Typically people go to bars and clubs not only in hopes of having a good time but also to meet other people. The problem with bars and clubs is it's often too loud to hear what the other person is saying. One way to overcome this is to use a time-honored approach known as the "taking a survey method."

In this classic but effective approach you bring a pen or pencil and a small notepad. I like this approach because it's fun and you don't have to say a word; just hand over the note and smile while doing it. Your note should say something like:

"Hi, I am taking a survey on the best pick-up lines. Please circle which one you *like* the best."

1) You bring fries with that shake?
2) Did it hurt when you fell from heaven?
3) Do you know karate, because your body is kickin'?
4) Hi, I'm taking a survey on bad lines.

The cornier the lines, the better, because they are bound to make her a laugh. Just remember to smile. If this doesn't work, move on. She's uptight and/or has probably got some drama in her life affecting her personality and willingness to have fun and relax. Bottom line is she is not going to be worth the effort.

A good trick for that girl you know and want to get to know better, or perhaps for that girl in the club, involves whispering in her ear. All you got to do is say *hi*, but the trick is, on your way to whispering in her ear, breathe warmly on her ear and neck to excite the very sensitive nerves there. Nothing perverted—just your normal breath. It should be done like it was not intentional and you wouldn't think she would notice it. Using flattery in this environment is actually okay here more so than other places. Girls like it—who wouldn't, right? Plus you have to keep in mind what she is wearing. If the outfit is showing off a lot of skin, she's there not only to show the other ladies that she too looks good but it's kind of an invite to guys to drop on by and say *hi*. Just be sure to keep it to one or two compliments. Any more than that and she is going to think you're trying too hard or into her for only one aspect of her, like her body. The flirty sexual tone of a flattering comment however shows confidence, guts/balls, and lots of girls like the direct approach. Just remember *they need you and don't overdo it.*

If you're going to hit on a girl in a bar, keep in mind human nature. Girls are not just at a bar/club to meet a guy. Yes, they may be open to it, but it is not necessarily their primary goal. Even if it is and they want to meet a guy, odds are she is not going to pick one and stay with one right away. There are too many guys running around and she will want to talk to as many as she can to find the right one for her. On top of this, a girl gets hit on and flattered by all the guys' comments over how hot she is. That's going to give her a big head and who doesn't like getting attention? If it was you, I bet you would love to have a small horde of women begging for your attention too. Very human, very normal.

The smart move here is to hold off introducing yourself until the time is right. Typically, that is when things have slowed down and the rush of men approaching her has slowed down to little or nothing. Then *ta-da!* You appear and you are "the one," but remember timing is really important. If you wait too long, like when things have slowed down and the bar is closing, guess what? She's going to be sleepy. Duh! That means she's going to bed, without you.

As you can see, there are a lot of potential problems at clubs or bars. This is why unless you're really good and willing to put in the effort, I suggest not trying to meet girls here. There really are far better and more effective places to meet women.

A word of advice on picking up women in clubs or in groups: don't try to pick up on the hottest girl there or pay most of your attention to her. The reason is that the other girls are going to know what you're up to. By not putting the majority of your attention on the hottest one, you're bound to make the one you want jealous. She'll be sitting there wondering why you're not trying to get with her like every other guy.

Speaking of picking up girls in a group, a great tactic is to go up and approach the one you want and start laying on the lines. I can practically guarantee you that one of her friends is going to get jealous and jump up in your face and tell you to get lost. When this happens, just smile and say, "Wow, I didn't think such mean (or ugly, depending on what she said) words could come out of such a pretty face."

Charm, my friend, will overcome most obstacles and get her friends to like you too. To a girl that's a very big plus. Now her friends will invite you to sit with them because they feel bad and like you now, or better yet they will leave you and their friend alone. Now you can proceed talking as you normally would.

Even if her friends jump in your face, so long as you say what I told you or some other charming line you can't lose. By being nice and polite to her friends you're showing her that you can be nice *despite* her friends being rude. That's going to earn you points along with her sympathy. If she doesn't tell her friends to shut up and go for you right there, she will probably come around to you in her own time later that night. If not, she's likely taken, gay, or both. They can't all be single and straight.

The Working Environment

Another difficult place to meet women is at her place of employment. You can use and change up the following lines at just about any restaurant, bar, or other place women work. Several people have told me different versions of this line, but they are always over-the-top compliments so I include one example of this line that is newish, and not overdone.

> Line: Excuse me, I just saw you from over there and I just wanted to tell you that every woman in this place is jealous of how sexy you are.

Sounds cheesy but it works because it is cheesy and some women like cheese. More importantly, it works because it appeals to basic psychology. First, everyone likes to be complimented so you can use this line even if a girl is not dressed up and in her work clothes. Second, women get dressed up and apply makeup for a few reasons such as to attract a man or to make themselves feel good. So few things beat being told you not only look good but that you look so good that you blow other women out of the competition and make them all jealous. After all, there is a level of completion between women in looks and looking for a man in a way. Just think of all the time and effort they put into getting dressed day in and day out. The likely response to that line is going to be "How do you know that?" You can play it off however you like, but I would suggest something like this: "Actually, I just wanted to give you a compliment so I could talk to you, but I bet I am right." You of course want to say this in a warm and friendly tone. Being honest, direct and not taking back the compliment makes you look brave and lets you stand out from the other guys who try to hit on her.

A variation on that line could be the following line.

Line: Smile and say, "Hey, I know you're busy at the moment, but I just had to tell you that you're really sexy and I just had to build up the courage to meet you." Ask her name and tell her your name and then excuse yourself back to whatever you were doing. All you have to say is, "Well, I will let you get back to what you were doing."

This line works because you're flattering her with how pretty you think she is and made it seem like she's so pretty that you just had to build up all that courage to meet her. By excusing yourself back to whatever you were doing, you made yourself an interesting curiosity for her. This approach puts the ball in her court, so if you don't want to make any more of an effort (at least at that time), you don't have to. It also lets her know you're interested so she doesn't have to worry about being rejected, but you are still making a bit of a challenge. Also, odds are she will be so flattered that when she gets the chance she is going to come over to you. This particular line is also a way just to get on someone's good side, and that can mean getting free stuff like extra coffee if she is working at coffee shop.

Both lines deserve special attention because they use the word *sexy*. Using the right words is a powerful tool in interacting with others. We will cover this more in another chapter. For now I point out the word *sexy* as a key word for you to use. The reason is a girl's mom, dad, grandmother, and friends all tell her how pretty, how cute, and even how beautiful she is, but not sexy. Sexy implies a desire, an attraction. By saying how sexy a women is, you're telling her that you find her attractive in a way that makes you stand out from other people, particularly other guys. It also has the effect of indicating that you don't want to be just friends, and finally, because it has the word *sex* in it, a person can't help but think of sex on some level. It's a good word; don't be shy in trying it. If you cannot muster up the courage to use it just yet, don't worry because you will at some point (probably at the end of his book). But alternatively you can try other things like "You're hot," "You are fine," "I find you very alluring," or "That perfume you are wearing is intoxicating." You can even try something kind of funny but dorky like "Excuse me, I just saw you and was like, *damn!* So I just had to build up the courage to meet you"

The word *sexy* does have a hidden bonus effect. If a girl is interested in you at all, she will thank you for the compliment. If she is not, she will step back, lean away, and say something like "Um, okay . . . thanks." And if those things happen it means she is not interested in you in that way . . . *yet.* The point is that using the word *sexy* allows you to figure out if she is interested in you. It is a nice way of figuring out where you stand with her without looking like you're insecure and saying something that sounds insecure. You can say other standard lines or compliments using the word *sexy*, such as "You look sexy today" or "You have a sexy smile" or "Those (pick an article of clothing) make you look sexy."

Using words like *pretty, cute* or *beautiful* are okay and can be effective too. Just keep in mind that if you want to make yourself standout and increase your chances, no word that I know of beats *sexy*. Go with what you like. The next few lines use these words so that you can try them out and change them up if you like.

Line: Wow (two-second pause), just wow. You are so pretty my brain shut off. That's the only word that I could think of when I saw you . . .

Line: Hi, I have a problem and I was hoping you could help me out. (She will say something.) Well, you see I have dinner reservations at (you pick the restaurant) for two but I need a second person. Care to help me out with that? (Smile.)

Line: You're great-looking, and I bet from the look in your eyes very sweet. And life is so unfair that you just have to be married, have a boyfriend, or both.

This wouldn't seem to work because you're basically calling her a whore and if she doesn't laugh (and most won't) you just respond with, "Well, I just figured you're so beautiful that any one man might not be able to handle you, but I am willing to give it a try," and then resume being your charming self.

Line: Hi, I lost my phone number. Can I borrow yours?

Line: Oh, your name's (insert name here). That's weird because that was the name of my last two girlfriends.

This implies that the third time is the charm and perhaps she's the one that you were meant to meet and be with. Some girls believe in fate and all that stuff. If they have an astrology tattoo the odds go up . . . astronomically.

Line: See my friend over there? He wanted to know if you think I'm cute.

You have to say this one properly with a tone of humor in your voice and a smile, or you can come off as insecure.

Line: If I had a nickel for every time I saw a girl as beautiful and you I'd have exactly five cents.

If she doesn't get this joke and figures out that a nickel is another way of having five cents, she's not overly smart.

Line: (You have to know the person's name and have met her once before) Hi (insert her name). I was just thinking what a beautiful day it is today but now that I have seen you it is perfect. (Emphasize the word *perfect,* and now smile.)

Line: (With brunettes only) Did you know that all the most beautiful women in history were brunettes? (She will say something.) Yep. Cleopatra, Aphrodite (a brunette historically, but turned into a blonde with Roman influence back in the days of Ancient Rome), and Helen of Troy were all brunettes.

Right there you have conveyed your smarts. You can then ask her what kind of guy she goes for. If she describes anything like you then you're good to go in and ask for a date. If what she says sounds nothing like you, simply turn it around and make a joke out of it. For example, you could say, using a warm, friendly and perhaps mildly sarcastic tone of voice, "Wow I am really close to that." Smile and ask her for a date. Your odds of getting a *yes* are much better if you display that kind of confidence and sense of humor.

There is seemingly an endless number of lines to use when meeting someone. You can pick them up from reading books, watching movies, or creating your own. This was just a short listing of ones that are not so common and fun to use. It's best to use one that you actually mean because sincerity is important.

Going Down with Dignity

Now there will be on the rare occasion the complete, and let's just say cold woman with problems, who is going to really rip into you without mercy and try to take the wind out of your sails. Maintain your dignity by refusing to lower yourself to her level. Whatever her reason for being just plain mean, here is how you shoot her right back down. The point of these tactics you are about to learn is not to get revenge but to get what you want.

Line: Thanks for showing me how classy you can be . . .

That one is my favorite; a friend told it to me. It points out her poor behavior.

Line: I can't believe such ugly words could come out of such a pretty face.

This one is the same line you can use when a girl's ugly friend jumps up in your face, as you recall, and works for similar reasons.

Line: Well, the loss is all mine, I'm sure.

This one is okay and I included it in the book because if you say it with the right tone you can come off as handling the situation in a nice way while still conveying an undertone of sarcasm that she or others around her may or may not pick up on. It has a slight flavor of that all important message of "I don't need you but you need me." I have actually had this line work and followed up by hugs and later kisses from apologetic women.

Line: I'm just a lonely Cancer trying to come out of my shell and you just slammed me back in it for the next few months.

You can vary this depending on your astrological sign. If you're a Scorpio, you're going back in your nest (eewww). If you're a ram or Taurus, you're going back into your barn, pen, and so on. It's also effective because you're telling them a bit about your supposed personality by mentioning your astrological sign, and this opens up the door for more conversation in case she or one of her friends happens to be into that sort of thing. A good indication of this is if they have a tattoo of their astrological sign.

A fun way to really piss off a girl that may still enable you to get her is to call her a name. I don't mean a mean name; I mean a nice name. Here's how you do it.

You: Right, well, see you around, baby.

Her: (if she responds, and she likely will) Don't call me *baby*.

You: Okay, see you around, honey.

Her: Don't call me honey either!

You: Whatever you say, baby.

Her: I told you not to call me that!

You: Right, right. I forgot, *baby.* (Smile.)

On the last response, you muster up all the humor you can and smile because she is now acting like a baby. She is going to be really pissed or realize that you were just stringing her along and laugh. If she laughs and you want to try it again, resume your pass.

You might ask yourself, *How can I advocate being mean back to a person in any way, shape, or form?* Well, I think of it as being necessary sometimes for a few reasons. First, some ladies won't give you the time of day until they know you are not some wimp and are mean to you to test if you're *man enough to handle them.* It's wrong, but that is how it goes sometimes. Second, and particularly if there are other people around, why should you stand there and take it and look like a clown for their entertainment? She's being the rude one and by saying something clever right back at her you are taking a stance that is a bit higher than her level while still standing up for yourself. This will increase your confidence, make you feel better, and—who knows?—it may even get you some respect from other people, both men and women alike. Notice that when you fire back, you don't have to be an ultra jerk. You can be nice, even funny, and still stand up for yourself.

Dog Fight

In aerial combat, when two planes go head to head, it's called a dogfight. The fight is over territory, and that hot lady that that guy came to the party with is going to be your *"territory"* soon enough. Obviously sneaking in on someone's date can be a difficult situation. The classic tactic here is to have a friend called a *wingman* pull the hot girl's friend or boyfriend aside, giving you room to angle in using one of your lines and conversational skills to get her number or better still to get her to leave with you.

I don't advocate stealing another guy's date or girlfriend. Using this tactic, you could do that, but that's not my intent. It is important to recognize, however, that just because a lady shows up with a guy does not mean she's with him romantically. He could be *a friend,* brother, or just on her first date and not having a very good time. You won't know unless you spot them holding hands or kissing, or just plain ask them.

A wingman is nice to have but you can win the fight without him. Here is how: Introduce yourself to the guy she is with and ignore her *almost* completely. Talk with him about whatever subject he wants to talk about that you can find out information on: his work, favorite sport, etc. It's easy because as you know by now, people love to talk and especially about themselves. Keep pretending to care about what he's saying, and buy them both drinks. He will eventually get so drunk he's going to make an ass out of himself scoring you points with his female companion as you continue to be nice. At some point, one of them is going to have to go to the bathroom. This is your chance to sweep in and get the girl. If he leaves, make your move fast; get her number and, win or lose, leave the party. You don't want her mentioning how you hit on her while he was gone because this is likely going to lead to a fight as well as possible jail time if you get busted for fighting. If she leaves, take a minute to say good-bye to the guy and head over to the ladies bathroom and hang about for a bit. When she comes out, make your move and then leave the party. Naturally this is best to do toward the end of the party or shortly before you want to leave anyways.

While we are on the subject of picking up women at parties, let's talk about the time-honored tactic of buying the girl at the bar a drink. *One of the most common mistakes men make is buying that pretty girl across the room a drink and assuming that her accepting* it somehow means she is obligated to speak with or dance with you. There's nothing wrong with buying a lady a drink. In fact, it can be an open-door invitation to them to come over and meet you, but how you do it is key. There are many variations on how to go about this, but I find this one to be the most effective.

There are two ways to go here. One is to note what she is drinking or ask the bartender if you are not sure. The other is just to buy her a drink when you see she has no drink in her hand. One way or the other, buy a drink and have the *bartender* deliver it, and make sure to tip him at least ten bucks to point out to her just who the guy is that bought her that drink. That's it. Going over and forcing a conversation is not the way to go. She needs you, remember? You need to be different from all the other guys. So just enjoy yourself, have a good time, and if she is single and interested she will come over on her own to you.

If you just have to introduce yourself, wait a few minutes after she accepts the drink and go over and make a pass. Just don't think that because you voluntarily bought her a drink you can be bothering her the rest of the night. If the connection is not there, move on. Who knows? She might tell one of her friends about the nice guy who bought her a drink and send her over your way. There are plenty of other fish in the sea, my friend.

From the Top

Another tactic to use when meeting people is to be aware and observe how they look. Try not to jump to conclusions based just on how they look. Instead, use your knowledge as a *reference* point to indicate what the person is into or what the person might be like. Let's start by pointing out a few common observational reference points by looking at people from the top down.

Hair styles changes constantly as time goes on, but there are a few constant rules of thumb that you can go by. If the hair and especially the bangs of a person hang over covering their forehead or face, it is *an indicator* that no matter how confident he or she may seem, that person is insecure in some way and as a result ends up choosing a hairstyle that covers or hides the face! This is huge because it gives you an automatic insight into that person's state of mind and vulnerabilities.

Manner of dress is an important factor but is less reliable than hairstyle. Typically the manner of dress a person has on can identify for you what social group he or she most identifies with. This gives you the opportunity to determine if you would have anything in common, or what kind of person he or she is (overly concerned with looks or attention seekers) without even speaking!

For men, the big tip-off that a girl wants you to look at her is tight, skimpy clothing with cleavage showing. If a girl is dressed provocatively and is showing a lot of cleavage, it's likely that she wants men to look and is possibly even looking for a man. It is, however, *a trap* and a trick. Her looks reel you in; if she's into you, she won't mind you taking a few glances at her body. The trick is, if you focus too much on her body, she will end up thinking you're a pervert, telling you her eyes are up on her face and not down there, and will think you're only interested in her for her body. This is why keeping eye contact is so important.

Turn the tables on her and make eye contact while speaking to her. It helps if you stare into her right eye or focus on her nose or mouth while talking to her. These are points on the face that psychology has identified as the best places to look to show someone you're looking at the face. She will be confused and interested in you because you're not falling for her tricky little trap like other guys. You actually seem to want to get to know her! What a surprise for her! Don't feel bad or worry if you do happen to take a look once or twice. In fact, do at least once so she knows for sure you are not gay. Just make it quick and move back to focusing on her face and the conversation you will be having.

A guy who wants girls to know he's single typically has tight shirts to expose his arm muscles and when sitting takes up a lot of room spreading his arms and/or legs out as if to declare his territory. This means if you are (and want people to know you are) looking, try doing/paying attention to one or more of the following . . .

Posture for males and females are surprisingly alike for the single person. Both men and women tend to stand taller, suck in their guts, push their chests out, and lift their chins ever so slightly when they themselves are on the hunt for a date. The stance is remarkably like that in the military. Women have another weapon to use: how they walk. That seductive hip-swinging walk is another indication they are single and/or looking for attention.

Next we move to facial expressions. I recommend picking up books on how to read facial expressions. They are all about the same. It's pretty important that you do this, as it will help you to pick up on nonverbal signs on what the person is really thinking or feeling. It never hurts to have a refresher course.

Finally we come down to the shoes a person has on. Loafers/slippers are for someone in a relaxed state of mind, boots are for an honest and/or often blunt kind of person, and tennis shoes are naturally an indication of a sports person, or at least someone who likes to run (unless they are a work shoes). Heels can mean she wants to be taller but large heals means she wants to attract the attention of a man. Flat shoes with style are an indication she's on the go and wants to be able to walk at this time.

Homework Assignment 3

Go out and observe people and if you chose to do so, interact with anyone you observed. Take notes of any clear and noticeable observations that match what you have just read, thought, or observed. Next, identify for yourself the observational qualities you found to be most attractive. In other words, what is it you tend to look for in women? Taking notes is useful when doing this because then you're doing something other than just staring at people and that makes it less likely that you will be noticed.

CHAPTER 8

Making the Date

"The closer you get to the lighthouse, the darker it gets."
-Japanese proverb

How to Ask Her Out

I like the above proverb because, just like darkness in the proverb, fear grows the closer you get to the girl you want to ask out.

It is now time to learn how to ask someone out. But before you go for it, *stop*. You must stop and ask yourself what kind of girl you are about to ask out. That will help you figure out how to ask her out. Take a second or two to think about what type of girl she is based on how she looks and what she's said to you so far. By type of girl I am referring to the very basic and general attitudes women have about dating. I don't feel bad about doing this because there are different types of men out there too.

The first type of girl we will call the *adventure*. The second is the 'challenge' and the third type is called the 'lost girl'. Learning the difference between the three is really something you need to go out and experience for yourself so you can get a feel for each type. The best way I can describe each to you is as follows. The adventure girl's the kind of girl who is fun, open, and willing to meet people (i.e., you). They are the best kind of girl to date. Very easy to ask out too. All you have to do is ask. Adventure girls are often very outgoing and have a variety of interests and hobbies. Dating them makes you feel like you're on an adventure (hence the name) and things will seem pretty clear and very fun to you when you date this type of girl.

Challenge girls are your more . . . challenging types of girls. Challenge girls expect to have it all, are high maintenance, and may think of themselves as princesses who truly believe they are God's gift to men. This means you will have to be up for the challenge of wining and dining them at great costs, both in time and money, just on the chance of getting to the next date. That chance will always be a small chance. This type of girl tends to think she deserves the very best in men and in material positions. Asking her out means having to sell yourself more. Any misstep in your interactions with her or a poorly chosen night on the town or gift could cost you the next date. So be sure to take pictures of the two of you so you get some good memories and visual references. Challenge girls are difficult to date, hard to please, and not much fun.

The worst of the worst in my opinion are the lost girls. At least with an adventure or challenge girl you know what you're getting yourself into and can work with it. Lost girls are just confusing as all hell and make men feel, well . . . lost. Dating this kind of girl makes men feel confused and unsure about what to do. In other words, you will feel lost dating a lost girl. It's really very difficult to know before going out on a date if your date is a lost girl or not. Lost girls kind of blend into the social dating world. Sometimes they have hobbies and friends and look more like adventure girls. Sometimes they can look and act like challenge girls. This means you have to date a few to get a feel for what a lost girl is. Perhaps the best way to tell before you ask a lost girl out is to scope her out a bit and see if she is the kind of girl that is very indecisive and tends to look at the world in a more negative than positive way. If you can see those two traits clearly enough in a girl then you might want to steer clear of her. Lost girls hurt a man's self-esteem the most among the three. Dating a lost girl is kind of like gambling; maybe you will hit the jackpot, maybe you won't. Just like real gambling, however, odds are you won't hit that jackpot and you will leave broke and brokenhearted, feeling lost, and confused. Happily, if you are really using this book like you are supposed to, you will at least get something out of it.

Go for an adventure or challenge girl and save yourself the effort and confusion of dating a lost girl. I want to warn you against some girls. Just like some guys, a girl can have such a poor mentality that they purposely or otherwise end up using members of the opposite sex. The best way to not get played is to just walk away. Even if you end up playing the player, you waste a lot of your time, effort, and possibly your money on something that just isn't going to be worth it.

A little secret between us though that ties back into the concept of telling a girl *no* is that walking away is just like telling a girl *no,* and it can result in her chasing after you. It's the same as if she was being rude to you and talking on the phone during your date. Remember to *charm, not chase.* Once you know you want to ask her out and are going to go for it, I suggest the following.

Perhaps the best way to ask a girl out on a date is to do it right then and there. Typically I go for a quick fifteen—to thirty-minute coffee (or whatever is close by) date the first time. This way you are not asking for a big time commitment. It's like a mini-date to get to know one another and requires less time and commitment for them. Spending a little bit of time on the spot is not such a big deal to ladies. It's a bigger deal if she has to take time to get dressed up and take time out of her day to plan on going out with you. A girl is a lot more likely to say *yes* to a mini-date after you meet her than to a full-on date. It's after the mini-date you want to ask for the full on date that would last a few hours. When you ask for an actual date, never ask them out for a first date on Friday or Saturday. Those are major days that she probably has plans on. In truth, in a girl's mind those are days that you should be busy too, at least when you first meet. Shoot for a weeknight instead.

She's into you or she's not. Move on if she's not interested in the mini-date or willing to meet up with you later. If you do get her number, some people would recommend holding off for a few days to a week before calling and asking for any kind of a date. Social dating rules advocate this and both work. Just looking at the odds and human factors, it does seem your odds of success go up by asking for a mini-date first.

Getting the phone number is simple: ask for it. There is not really an easy or slick way to go about it other than using the other tactics you have learned so far (tone of voice, humor). You can of course vary how you say it. I like to say, "You know I'd like to take you out sometime and get to know you better. Can I get your number?" This tells her you're interested but not gaga over her and just want to explore the possibility of getting to know her better for friendship, sex, love, or romance.

Getting her number is a clear sign that she likes you on one of those levels. Otherwise she wouldn't give you her number.

If you don't want to run the risk of coming off as some poor slob, or a throwback to the caveman days, you need a cell phone. The old pen and paper routine is out. Pen and paper should only be used in emergencies. Not having a phone might make you not only look poor but unreachable as well. In an on-demand world and in a world where both guys and girls seem to be more open to cheating on one another, your not having a phone looks bad. A girl's going to want to know at some point in a relationship that she can contact you the minute she needs you.

The rules for text messaging on a phone are the same as for e-mails. You will read up on that in another chapter. For now, just don't do it.

Once you have the number, leave. You want to leave the girl thinking about the great, somewhat mysterious guy she just met. If you stick around you might say something stupid. Women like the idea of going out with this stranger who seems nice but that they don't really know. I think it provides them an element of danger and an "anything might happen" sense of excitement.

One thing to add once you have the number is to say you need to meet up with some people or friends. It's good to say this because it lets her know on some level that you do have a social life, you have friends (meaning some people like you), and you won't be overly dependent on her. Finally, because you have friends (or say you do), you provide the opportunity for meeting new people and can at least become a social outlet for her. Add it all up and you make yourself and your chances of your first phone call going much better. Remember she needs you and not the other way around!

Unfortunately, sometimes a girl is just too shy to tell the truth or thinks she is being nice and letting you down easily by giving you a fake number. Or better still, you might get the "I don't have a phone" line. If this happens, oh well. She was trying to let you down easily or hoping you'd get the hint. Bottom line in today's world of computers, cells, and house numbers: if she honestly didn't have a phone, she would offer some kind of method for you to contact her if she was interested in you. If she doesn't offer any way to contact her, take the hint and move on.

Sometimes you get a fake number, call, and then . . . surprise! It's not her number. If you're lucky enough to see that "fake phone number" person again, just play it off. Say *hi* to her as if she wasn't the immature girl that you know she is and tell her you lost her number or forgot to call, but *do not ask for it or another date again.* Just ask how she's doing. She will respond and all you have to say is, "Cool. Well, I got to get going. See you soon." She will be standing there wondering if you really lost her number and didn't care enough to ask for it again or not. You get to mess with her head, just like she tried to do to you, and walk away with some dignity.

The Phone Call

When asking a girl out on the phone, your tone of voice and rate of speech are going to be important factors. You want to do two things when calling: make going out with you sound *fun,* and appeal to her curiosity. As a side note, you can do this when asking her out in person too. This doesn't mean you have to do anything other than dinner and a movie. You're a nice, funny guy and naturally you just need to get her to believe that in order to get her to say *yes*. Here is how it should go about it:

You: Hey, how you doing?

Her: "Good, how are you?"

You: Great, glad to know you're good. (This is important because it tells her you care about how she feels on some level, or leave it out if you think that's being too nice.) I was just calling because I have some free time and wanted to get together. Figure we can go out and have some *fun* (put the right inflection on the word *fun*) and I have a surprise for you too. How about this Thursday night at seven?

You want to mention that you're using your free time and not that you're making some special arrangements to go out with her. You want to make a date and time that works for you because it shows that she's working on your time. If you ask what day works for her, you come off as weak and overly considerate and that, sadly, almost never scores you any points. After asking, shut up and look at your watch and count out three seconds. If she doesn't say "Sure" or something to that effect, you're in trouble and not likely to get the date, unless you do some fast talking and try selling yourself. One thing you can do that works well is turning her doubt and hesitation into a positive like so:

You: (adding on to your last comment.) Oh, and I promise that if you don't laugh at least half the time we are out I'll refund all your money. (Pause one second.) Come to think of it, since you don't have to spend any of your money you have nothing to lose (light chuckle).

This way you are pointing out in a nice way that she has nothing to lose and shouldn't be so concerned about the whole thing.

Her: That sounds great what are we going to do?

At this point you have to watch yourself. You do not want to offer to do whatever she wants to do because that makes you come off as either indecisive or a pushover. Pick at least one thing you're going to do and if you feel like it offer to let her pick one thing she wants to do. Normally you don't do that, but I like to offer to them to pick something that they will enjoy just to show I don't always have to do what I want. You can save that option for the other dates if you like.

So you're surprised. What's it going to be? Well, it can be anything you want. Take her to play laser tag or skating. Heck, take her to Europe if you can afford it. Just keep in mind that the bigger the surprise, the more she's going to expect down the road. Personally, I like to start small. Dinner, some fun activity, and, for the surprise, some small tiny gift. I like to get something that reminds me of her. (For example, say she likes Betty Boop, that old black and white cartoon character.) You can also pick something up on that date to commemorate it, like a postcard (possibly one with Betty Boop?), keychain, or other kind of knickknack, something under five bucks. Sounds bad, or cheap, but if you do it right, make it something small and thoughtful—explain it if you have to. She will appreciate it. One of the best things you can do in this area is to pick up origami (Japanese paper folding) as a hobby. It's simple, neat, and cheap, but thoughtful because you had to put some effort into it. You can even show her a magic trick you learned and it won't cost you dime. Plus it provides a sense of wonderment. But let's get back to the phone conversation.

You: Well, I thought we'd go to this great little restaurant I know called blah, blah, blah . . . The food is great.

Her: Sounds great. I'll see you at seven.

Now there is the possibility that she won't want to go out with you because something else has come up or you didn't make yourself sound worthy enough of her time. Here is how to recover.

Her: Well that sounds okay, but I have to go blah, blah, blah . . .

You: Right, well, guess we will have to try some other time in the week then.

At this point she could just let you go or make you a counter offer. This last line opens up the conversation to give her that opportunity to make a counteroffer. Some women just like to string guys along to build up their self-esteem. Sick, huh? If she says good-bye, let her go, toss her number, and move on.

If she really is busy but wants to go out with you she will make a counter offer.

Her: Oh, well. I can't at all this week but next Thursday night at eight would be okay.

Don't fall for this trap. Even if she were to make you a counteroffer for the next day, much less next week, say *no!* Remember saying *no* puts you in control and makes her want you that much more. Plus accepting makes you seem too easy, eager, and available.

You: That sounds great, but unfortunately I can't. I have some important stuff I need to do.

You can add on . . . for your family, if you think it will score you points. This depends on the girl.

You: How about we do Thursday at five instead?

Or

You: How about we do Monday instead, say six o'clock?

Her: That will work I'll see you then. You can pick me up at . . .

Okay so now you have established you're no pushover and, most importantly, you have given her a taste of the fact that *she needs you,* and *you don't need her!* That, my friend, is a bad human flaw we all have—the need to be wanted and needed by others.

Occasionally you will run across an evil woman who will inform you that she will give you her address when you call back before you come pick her up, or that you should call her thirty minutes before you come over and confirm that one of you hasn't had a change in plans. She may even try the old "I don't make plans because they always seem to get broken" line to avoid making a commitment for a date. Both are classic lost-girl moves. When this happens, it means one of two things. First she likes you enough to give you her number but not enough to actually go out with you, at least at this time. Second, it could mean that she's got some other guy she's more into on the side and is waiting to see how things play out with him first. When this happens, just move on. Tell her it sounds like she has a lot going on and you will call some other time when her schedule's not busy. Hold off calling back for seven to eight days and try again. If she tries the same line again, toss her number and move on. She is just wasting your time and you may end up wasting your money.

When the timing is off and you can't work out a date reasonably quickly, there are essentially two options.

1) Tell her that you will try again when her schedule's not so busy. The hidden meaning is she being too uptight about this. A date is just a date after all. It's not like you're asking for a lifetime commitment.

2) Tell her, "Well, this is just how I like to do things when I call or make a date with someone and something has come

up. I leave it up to them to call/make the next date. If you
want to go out, I am interested. Call me."

I like option two best because it conveys several important
messages. The first is that you don't need her. The second is you
won't be controlled or manipulated into trying again, and hence
you're a challenge. Third it leaves it up to her to call but makes it a
safe guarantee that you will indeed say *yes* if and when she does.

You may be surprised at the startlingly frequency of girls who
do indeed call back at anytime from a few days to months later
asking if you still want to "hang out sometime."

It's a nice surprise for you and if she never calls back you know
she's not interested and can move on without making an idiot out
of yourself.

Never Ask Any Girl Out More Than Twice

A girl may say *no* to you the first time you ask her out or for
her number. If you really like this person, wait a few weeks and
make another pass at her. If she still says *no,* regardless of what she
says to you it means that something is going on with her or in her
life that *could* have nothing to do with how she feels about you
and the bottom line is she's not interested right now. Just move on.
Believe me it's never a good idea to get involved with people who
have more problems than you do. Whatever her reasons, moving
on keeps you from looking and indeed being some desperate guy.

A bad habit that people, particularly men being the social
protectors that we are, tend to make is excuses for people. We
say to ourselves, *Well, she just wants to me to confirm or whatever
because she's been hurt in the past or she's just being careful.* Honestly,
this could be true, but look at it like love is a risk. If you're not
willing to take the risk, don't play. It's pointless as guys to get hung
up on one girl or on *what could be* and is one of the biggest reasons
nice guys turn into stalkers.

At this point in the book you should already have an attitude
that makes getting stuck on one girl very unlikely. I point it out

here now so that you don't waste your time playing some game with a girl who is clearly not ready to date. And just to be clear, it's not your job or responsibility to help her get ready to date. Just move on.

Computerized Communications

These next few sections address rules and etiquettes for messages and when to leave them. This part can be very complex.

In today's world with caller ID, if you call and call without leaving a message you're going to come off as a stalker. Calling once every day is not okay either. The best way to get a hold of someone is to ask when she is normally free to talk because girls love to talk on the phone, and they are generally happy to tell you when you can call. If you missed the boat on gathering that information, call once in the afternoon from one to three (typical lunchtimes at work) or once at night from 7-9 (typically right after dinner and TV time). If you didn't get a hold of her, do not call again for two or three days. Then try it again. If she has not returned your call by looking at her caller ID then you may as well leave a message at this point, *if* you don't normally see this person. Perhaps she thinks your number belongs to a telemarketer trying to sell birdseed. If you *do* normally see this person in your week-to-week activities then just go for it and ask her out in person, even if by her non-responsiveness the odds seem against you. You will never know unless you try.

As a general rule you do not want to leave a message with her machine or anyone else for that matter. The reasons are simple. You will likely sound like an idiot on a machine because in the course of conversations people (this means you) tend to say things like um, ah, and so . . . This can make you sound like a mental case, a high school dropout dumb-dumb. It is not so bad when you're having a conversation with the other person live on the phone or in person because she is processing what you said *and thinking of what to say next.* So she largely misses those verbal errors. Plus some girls will play the message over and over analyzing it and sitting around asking friends to do the same. That's weird and bad for you.

Leaving a message with mom or the roommate is a no-no also. People tend to screw things up when second-handedly relaying a message and may even forget to tell the person your message. More importantly, you can't see her facial expressions, read her tone of voice, or use your voice skills by leaving messages.

If the wrong person is picking up the phone and the person you want to talk to is not home, just ask when she will be home. Most people will tell you. If someone asks who you are, say you're a new friend and ask when she will be home. In an absolute worst-case situation, go ahead and leave your name and number only, but only do this on the third attempt and don't expect to get called back.

Texting, instant messages via face book and e-mail are very popular methods of conversation for girls. Now as a general rule repeat after me: "I will not text, e-mail, or leave a message of any kind for a girl before the third date." Let's try that again: "I will *not* text or e-mail or leave a message of any kind for a girl before the third date."

The reason is simple, even if you have known the girl for years (at work for instance). *You're playing a different game now* and she is looking at you like someone who has potential for her. Sending a text or e-mail does not let you use your tone of voice or any other skills that you have and the text/e-mail itself will be open to her interpretations and her own mental voice. Meaning she won't hear your voice in her head saying all the right things in all the right ways.

Internet Dating

I have to confess my expertise is lacking when it comes to Internet dating. The upside to this method of dating is that you get to pick and choose who you are interested in and even get to know a little about them before ever meeting them. The rules are simple and the knowledge you gained so far in this reading can be applied to the Internet.

There are however, a few key things to keep in mind.

1) Don't log on to your site every day. Most sites keep a record of when you last logged on. Every two to four days is acceptable. More than that and you can be seen as being too busy for a relationship. If you log on every day, you run a high risk of someone noticing it and your apparent desperation to meet someone.

2) Don't put up photos of your nieces and nephews if you're looking for a date. There are so many people online that a person would have to be unemployed in order to read all the profiles. Typically people look at photos first and if they see a kid or baby they are likely to assume it's yours and move on. Doing so is okay, but just remember you are shooting yourself in the foot and significantly lowering your chances of meeting someone. Instead, how about you just put in your profile how cute your sister's or brother's kids are and how much you love them.

3) No one really cares about how much you drank or what it was, so avoid the booze photos unless it was at a special party/event. Instead use photos of yourself doing things you enjoy: travel, hiking, riding your motorcycle, etc . . . That way they can imagine themselves doing those things with you.

4) Keep your profile short but informative. You don't want to give everything away before they even meet you. Typically, that means two to three paragraphs.

5) Online communication gives the illusion of this great person you can meet out there. It's a hopeful fantasy to keep people going. Don't expect to meet everyone in person and don't ask to meet before the third communication.

6) When you do ask, just mention how you don't want to be overly pushy but that you like what you know about them so far and would like to meet up with them in person this Wednesday at 1 PM for coffee (or whatever you want, so long as it's in public). Include that if she thinks it's too

soon you understand and won't ask again until she's ready because you don't want to be pushy. Women appreciate that you recognize the potential for danger in meeting online. As this form of dating improves over time in our society, the worry won't be as concerning.

CHAPTER 9

Planting the Seeds of Love and Lust

"Love is of all passions the strongest, for it attacks simultaneously
the head, the heart, and the senses."
~ Lao Tzu

Sensory Recall

One horrible thing everybody has done at one time or another
is mention their exes on a date. True, you could shut them
down and take charge and tell them you would rather not hear
about that. It can be a turn-on and may result in after hours
activities with you because she will be more aware of the issue and
want to prove to herself she is over her ex. As a bonus, ladies will
recognize you're not some weak guy.

Using sensory recall on a date can be very risky and produce
feeling of love for an ex-boyfriend, but if you want to give it a try
here is how it basically goes. Ask the other person to play along
and recall the last time they had fun. Ask them: What were you
doing? Was it a hot day out? What sounds were around you? What
smells were there? How did you feel? This is a good but somewhat
tricky way of getting someone in a better mood and brings her
mental awareness to that recall moment. Hopefully the memory
was not with her ex.

The other way to handle this, or if you have the balls to bring it up, is ask about her last/best/most fun sexual experience. Why would you do that? Simply by asking her about it and asking questions like the ones you just read, you are forcing her to relive, in part, that experience. This, my friend, is like finding that kink in the proverbial armor and is a great way to not only find out more about her but also to help get her in the mood. As a warning, this does have the potential to backfire and send her back to her ex. You have to use your own best judgment here on her and how things are going on your date.

Other senses you can play off of include the following and should also be used in building romance as well.

Taste

Ask yourself what you can serve up, or where can you go that she will enjoy. What's her favorite food? Does she or will she eat any foods that are known to be aphrodisiacs, such as oysters or strawberries dipped in chocolate? Go on and create a list of them and buy what you can afford and feed them to each another. Remember to have fun and be lighthearted—it's a fun night for you too. Just be sure to not get too much whipped cream on her nose as you clumsily try to feed her that strawberry.

Touch

How soft or comfortable are the chairs? You are not wearing anything that might feel rough against her skin, are you? Let's not forget the to fluff up the pillows and use a high thread count for the bed sheets just in case you end up there at the end of the night.

Sight

Blaring, bright lights, not so romantic. Soft, dim white light (think candles if you want), that's romantic and appeals more to the senses. For the record, so are hanging bed curtains if your bed can have them. Remember it's about the atmosphere.

Smell

Smelling your dirty laundry, not sexy or romantic. Do your laundry and stash it out of sight. Use scented candles and an air freshener of her favorite flower, or better yet real flowers. That's romantic.

Sound

Music is always good. Slow romantic music or music you know she likes is good too. Your heavy metal music, probably not. Music is however a deeply personal thing and when your date/girlfriend hears the music she is going to tie it to her memory of the moment—who you are as a person—and it's going to appeal to her on some emotional level. As you can see, music is a powerful thing. So you really need to consider how long and how well you know this person and what message or mood you're trying to set when you play music. Don't just put anything on, put some effort into the selection.

Word Dropping

Using the right word or words in a conversation can produce amazing results. For instance, she's talking and talking on and on about what a tough time she's having at work. You can respond, "Sounds like you're having a pretty *hard* time. It must make you pretty *tense* having to go to work day in and day out." In this example you planted the word *hard* (as in *my penis is hard,* and *tense* as in you might want to have sex to relieve all that tension) into your responses. You have to be careful of this one because you don't want it to be obvious, so your tone of voice and the inflection you give to these words are important. Done properly, you will oh-so-sneaky-like bypass her defenses and get her thinking what you want her to think.

There are so many words to use in this manner (remember the word *sexy!*) but here are a few basic and easy ones with examples on how they might fit into a conversation.

Words to use

Hard: It was a hard day at the office today.

Moist: The air outside feels pretty moist.

Penetrate or penetrating: That's a very penetrating question. I am glad you asked it.

Wet: It's really wet outside today, isn't it?

Firm: You have to firmly but gently pet the dog in order to gain its full trust.

Stimulating or arousing: This has been a very stimulating conversation.

When Words Fail

So you're at her place hanging out or on the date and an incoming call makes its way to her phone. Guess what that is. It's likely to be her escape excuse. She may say there is an emergency that has come up, and she's really sorry but she has to go. Yeah, right. If she doesn't like you, it's an emergency. If she does, it's her friend who she will talk to later. Some people have no manners, however, and rather than turn the phone off, not answer it, or keep the call short, they sit there talking and talking. If not on purpose, you can at least use this to your advantage. Wait no more than three to five minutes and do one of the following.

1) Get up, put some money on the table if needed, wave, and walk away. I guarantee she going to hang up, apologize, and ask you to stay. Now she knows she's dealing with a man that she can't walk all over. Big turn on for them and points for you.

2) When she finally gets off the phone, be mean (assuming the conversation she was having wasn't about her mom or dad being in the hospital, etc.). Be mean, tell her the truth. Tell her in a mean, aggressive tone that you do not appreciate being ignored and how she should be ashamed for treating someone like that on a date. Doesn't she know any better? Doesn't she have any common sense, any manners? Get up and walk out. If she's sick enough to try this with you, the odds are good (after you let her have it) she will almost magically be in love with you.

I include that little tactic in this part of the book and in this chapter because it is one little thing you can do that will let her know you are not a pushover. From there she will respect you and once you have that, love is more likely to grow.

CHAPTER 10

Where to Get a Date and Where to Take Your Date

"Even the greatest strategy is useless in the hands of a coward."
~Unknown

A Date Is Just a Moment in Time

It's very important to note that just because you see a hot girl, it doesn't mean you have to make a move on her or even talk to her for that matter. So long as she has noticed your presence around her, you become part of a familiar backdrop to her. You can hold back a few times then introduce yourself. That way you don't come off as some horny guy trying to have sex with the first girl (and every girl after) that he meets.

Homework Assignment 4

While it is theoretically possible to meet someone at any time and in any place, you can improve your odds by meeting someone who travels in your social circles of friends and who is interested in the same things you are. For instance, oftentimes people meet at a friend's party and the person you meet may be a friend of a friend.

Perhaps you will meet a person that you would like to go out with at church or a club meeting.

You assignment is to seek out a church or club or other kind of venue/hobby that you enjoy and can meet people at. Keep in mind that it is not necessary for you to instantly ask someone out. The fact that you share membership or a common interest at some place practically guarantees that you will see her again at some point. So why not take your time and get to know the other person, and then ask her out in a group setting first, or one on one in a friendly manner. This allows for the two of you to get to know one another and determine for yourselves if there is potential for a dating relationship.

As a side note, I recommend that you have a hobby that involves no members of the opposite sex and allows you to relax and take your mind off members of the opposite sex. Being a group member is a great way to meet people, make friends, and meet someone special. There are many clubs and groups to join that can be found in newspapers, local libraries, fitness clubs, and places listed online. Just try looking.

Note: Joining a poker club or something where you don't have to interact with anyone face to face and in person, like an online club, is not the goal here.

It's just one date, after all, and as you have learned this far you don't need to panic. There are plenty of women in the world; if something goes out of whack, it's not the end of your entire dating life.

Let's review. So far, you have learned how to build confidence and how to communicate, among other things. But how do you get from point A (knowing how to use these skills) to point B (where and when to use them on a date)? Just where do you put your new talents to use?

Places to Meet Women

Remember it is possible to meet someone at any time and in any place. This is just a listing of common places where girls hang out.

Gift card or food sections at stores

Takes a bit of skill to strike up a conversation, but you can do it now. Just make a comment on the card she is looking at or the food she is going to buy. You can even ask where some food item is even if you really know it's on lane 8. Just remember to compliment and not criticize. If you complain of prices or difficulties in finding whatever, you will be seen as a negative and somewhat unattractive kind of guy.

School, the ideal place

You may have a class together but, if not, you can easily start a conversation by asking her what subject she's into, what she majors in or hopes to major in, and what she wants to be when she grows up (in other words, her dream job). Plus on a lot of campuses, girls are just there to find a guy with a big wallet and big giving heart to marry.

Places of eating

Really, unless she's working there, meeting a woman in this setting is not the best place, but I include it here because if you eat out a lot and see women eating alone you might as well go for it. The reason being is that by and large humans, and especially girls, are social creatures, meaning most of the time people would prefer to not eat alone. If you just have to introduce yourself and she's with a friend, make your move but get out as fast as you can with her number. Just wait a few minutes to make sure her boyfriend or husband is not in the restroom and about to return.

Parties and bars

I have to tell you that it is not just women but men who sometimes need a little alcohol in them to bring down those defensive walls that keep the fun locked down. Drinking and partying has been going on for thousands of years, and if you agree then you already have an *in* as this lowers inhibitions. I can tell you that if a girl is not into me enough to be with me, stone sober, then no sex for her, but that's just me. Don't let that stop you. *Be sure to not drink more than one or two beers yourself.* This is one of the biggest mistakes guys make on a date. Whether the guys are drunkards or just nervous, the result is the same. The drunk and stupid guy often loses the girl. If you don't believe me, just watch some of those dating TV shows. Know what your limit is and keep your head.

Dancing

Another time-honored tradition. Dancing in and of itself works because you have an excuse to be around her, show her what you got, and hopefully make some kind of skin contact. All of it ups the odds in your favor. A popular myth that women mistakenly believe in is that how well a guy dances indicates how well he performs in bed. So learn how to dance (or don't and prove her wrong), and it wouldn't hurt to pick up a how-to-video for the sex department. That way you can prove her right.

Remember to be honest. Don't try something you know you're not good at. If you suck at dancing and have not worked at it, don't lie and say how great you are. Tell her you're not that experienced at it but for her you will give it a shot. She will think it's sweet and likely will dance with you. Even if you don't end up getting the girl, it's better than standing on the wall all night, so dance and have some fun.

Places of waiting

Lines are everywhere: at the bus stop, banks, grocery stores, DMV, etc. What's wrong with some pleasant side conversation? Nothing.

Singles clubs/speed dating

Sad places with regular meetings, but, hey, you never know. Plus they are all single and apparently have such bad luck with or meeting men that they are willing to take a chance, perhaps on you. By virtue of you're reading this, I know you're the kind of good guy who is looking to improve himself and I bet not just in the dating department. So I don't have to feel bad about letting a wolf into the sheep's pen now, do I? Actually, now that I think about it, might be equally possible you're the sheep entering the she-wolf den!

Bookstores and libraries

This place lets you check out what she is into reading for conversation, romance, self—help, etc. It is also an opening to your introduction even if it's something unrelated to what she's looking at. For example, at the library you can say, "Excuse me, I have not been here in a while. What way to D47.36?" After she responds, say, "Thanks, that's a nice necklace you have by the way." And now tie this into what you have learned so far and resume your advance.

A cruise

Take a vacation for yourself and if you happen to meet someone, all the better.

Stuck at the Laundromat?

So is she. Say *hi*. Ask her advice on what to put in your wash, even if you already know the answer.

The bus

I hate the bus. You probably hate the bus, but you know what? Some cuties ride the bus, and while you're there you can make some side conversation and use your skills to land her number. Just remember to get off the bus once you get the number.

At the pool

Ah, the pool. A great place to scope out ladies. A little shallow I know (pool = shallow = pun), but if they like how you look, your chances go up. They go up in part because you have seen them in their bikinis and have a pretty good idea what they look like out of their bikinis, and in part because you just might be touching those exposed parts . . . in the pool while you pick her up and dunk her in the water.

Volunteer activities

You like to help the animals, save the environment, give blood, and believe that you can swing the vote in your party's favor? Of course you do. Why not meet someone doing this kind of stuff?

The gym

You are fit . . . or at least you're working on it being fit, and she is fit. The endorphins are pumping for you both and this biochemically speaking makes people happy, feel all good, and glow inside. So go for it.

In a park or at a zoo

Nice day out playing fetch with the dog. See that girl and her dog playing fetch? Make a move. It's also a very nice day to go to the zoo and perhaps meet someone reading about the gorillas. Also a great place for a date if she likes animals.

A clothing store

This is a really fun one to use when you want a new look and have to go buy some new clothes. If you are like most guys, you find it very difficult to go shopping for clothes. Instead, try approaching that cute floor helper and tell her that you need a new look, but like most guys you just can't decide. Ask her if she were to go out with you what she would like to see you wearing. All you have to do then is let her pick out some clothing (it's okay to say *no* if she picks out something that's just not your style at all), make some conversation, and then ask her out. Since she just spent some time getting to know you and picking out clothes, she might just say *yes.* Even if she were to say *no,* at least you got some nice-looking clothes.

Work

Work is the number one place people meet and end up with future husbands and wives. Generally it's not a good thing to date where you work. Lots can go wrong, including you getting fired.

It happens a lot, however, because you see the person all the time and you have something in common.

Church

Church gets special attention for several reasons. Some people frown on looking for a date at church, but in reality the church wants you to meet people for dating there! Think about it: a lot of churches have services for people of the same age group. Just what other reasons might there be for the *sharing of the peace,* you know that part in church where you get to meet everyone and shake hands. What possible reason is this done for? True in part, it is so there is a sense of community, but it's also true that the church leaders want you to find love. They want you to meet someone; they want you to fall love and get married. Not just because they want you to be presumably happy but also if you have kids that's another member of the congregation right there! Church has a built-in introduction system for you and provides you with a chance and reason to make friends, as well as scope out potential dates, and it provides a reason to speak to them! Hard to ask for more than that. Plus spotting couples in church is pretty easy as they typically sit right next to one another, hold hands, and whisper to one another during the sermon.

Once you have someone who catches your interest, all you have to do is go back up to her, tell her you're new, and ask if she would be willing to talk over a cup of coffee or tea about the church and what it's like or maybe something non-church related.

Unless she's a repressed church girl waiting to have sex as soon as she can get it, figure on going in for the long haul on this one. Odds are you won't be getting any till the third to fifth date at least, if not longer. One way or the other, you can always see them again and meet new people next Sunday.

Compliments to Give Out

Both boys and girls alike love compliments. Aside from how big her breasts are or how great in bed she was, try out these little ones that might earn you similar compliments about your size and performance down the road.

Eyes: windows to the soul and all that.

Hair: very shiny and/or soft.

Clothing: "Pretty blouse you have there. I like the color." Or, "You look sexy in that."

Smile: "You have such a bright smile." "Your smile lights up a room." Go with these and make them your own. Just remember to use the proper tone of voice.

Additionally I recommend memorizing a few poetry lines. So pick up a book of poetry. You never know—it might come in handy. You don't need to go all out and be a goofy poet guy, but a few lines here and there placed on the occasional date as a compliment make you smart, romantic, and a tad sexy. Poetry works for some and not for others. It depends on what you say, so it's better to use your own best judgment depending on the situation. Don't feel bad if she doesn't like what you have to say. Part of using your own best judgment is doing what you think is fun and cool and if she doesn't, too bad for her.

Homework Assignment 5

Sit and think for a moment on the kinds of people that seem to get all the best dates. A few that might come to mind include:

- The pretty girl.
- The jock.
- The cheerleader.
- The pimp.
- The bad boy.
- The rich person.

I don't advocate that you try to become one of those kinds of daters. I simply want you to recognize that people are different and that regardless of what kind of style you have as a dater, there are certain key elements found between the most successful daters that we will identify and strive to emulate. The great news is at this point in the book you have significantly improved on these key skills. They are:

- Projecting confidence.
- Having interest in other things that establish your individuality.
- Having a sense of danger or being around entertainment (e.g., join a rock climbing club or a band, practice martial arts or at least say you do).
- Showing a sense of humor.

Like a cook's recipe, you need to be aware of these things within yourself. If you want, try identifying and writing a two-page, double-spaced paper on what your style is and what you can do to improve in one or more of the listed qualities. Then work on it.

Preparations for the Big Date

Short of a shower, being clean and well-groomed (I sincerely hope you know how to do that), remember to get the wax out of your ears with a Q-Tip.

Make sure you have a full tank of gas in your car. You want to provide the image of a guy who is always at his best and not a quart low.

Know how to get from point A (your house) to point B (her house) to point Z (where you're going for your date).

Plan it all out in advance.

Make sure you have enough cash in your wallet and expect her to sneak a peek in it. Have at least a fifty or a hundred-dollar bill strategically placed if she's going to be that kind of girl. She may think you're going to spend all that extra money on her at least some day. Like magic, it's probably an illusion, but she can think however she wants.

Paying for everything on the first date is something I like to do because I asked her out and she said *yes*. To me, that makes her my guest. I think this is how it should be, but let's face it: always doing that can leave you broke and feeling taken advantage of. So after the third date (or before, if you have slept with her), if she has not offered to pay for herself or you, start telling her that if she wants to go, she has to pay some of the cost. Alternatively, you pay one date and she pays the next. Just be sure to spend a little bit more on her than she does on you, or you will seem cheap and she will feel taken advantage of.

Additionally, always at the very least be ready to hold the doors open for your date on the way into any building. You just can't forget to do this so keep it in mind. If you don't hold the door open for your date, you are going to be perceived as less respectful toward her and that is going to likely lower your chances.

Since we're talking about doors, another aspect of a date is walking a girl to her door. Unless you have made arrangements to meet some place and she has her own transportation back home, plan on getting out of your car and walking up to her door to meet her at the start of your date and walking her back to her door at the end of the date. If she has a car and met you some place, you must at least walk her back to her car.

If you're picking her up at home, I suggest calling first and saying something like, "Hi, I am almost at your place. Do you want me to meet your parents/friends and come up to your door or just wait outside?" The reason I advise this is because some girls may not want you to meet the parents or friends for fear that it is too soon or their parents or friends might not like you before she decides if she really likes you. If that is the case, just open the car door when she comes out. If your date lives alone, just go to her door.

At the end of the date you should go to the door, and what to do next can be a bit tricky. You will want to observe her behaviors as well as what she says. If she says she had a nice time, that is a point. If she lingers at the door, plays with her hair, or flips her hair over one shoulder, or is fiddling with her keys, drops her keys or does any number of things, that means she is not rushing into the house to get away from you. It probably means she is hoping for a good-night kiss. Refer to the chapter on kissing, and good luck.

Some people advocate going in for the kiss but stopping about an inch away from her lips and holding there. The idea is that if you stop at this distance, it is not overly forceful and leaves it up to her to participate in the kissing. I think for some guys it probably works.

Personally, I advocate not planning on a first-date kiss. What I used to do at the girl's door was make a joke about it. I would say something like, "I would kiss you but I don't want you to think I am cheap (smile—it is a joke) but I did have a good time with you." This has the effect of showing respect for the awkwardness of the situation and her. Most importantly it has the effect of conveying the message that you're not so into her and thus don't need her. You will be able to tell from her reaction if she is wants or wanted that kiss. I advise not doing it and saving it for later. That way you become a challenge for her. However, if you want it badly and believe she does too, you can go for it by following up the last statement with something like this: "On second thought, I guess I can take a chance on you, but . . . I hope you will respect me in the morning." Smile and toss in a light chuckle. Then go in for the kiss. Saying things like that open up doors for you because you're showing her you're willing to be vulnerable but have a sense of humor about it. This means she is probably going to be less likely to turn down the kiss. Don't skip ahead in the book, but chapter 11 will cover more on kissing.

Where to Now?

As stated before, you can meet someone at any time and in any place. These are not only places to possibly meet someone, but also places to go on a date.

Far and beyond, lounges are my favorite places to meet women and go for a date for several reasons. I like them because they are not as loud as bars. The lighting is good and that makes both of you look good. Overall, it's mellow so you both can relax, she can drink if she wants to, the seats are soft and comfortable, and you can use your verbal and listening skills! You can of course start there and go someplace else after a bit.

Depending on your budget, you could go all out or be cheap and go somewhere inexpensive, or perhaps do a little bit of both for a date. I like balance and a middle of the path approach. It shows that you're not broke but that you're not the kind of person that needs money to have fun. You pick for yourself, but here are some places to go and things to do on a date that are typically best.

Dinner and/or a movie

Dinner and/or a movie deserve special attention here. Somehow dinner and a movie became socially accepted as a standard first date. I advise avoiding dinner for the first date. Possibly even the second. I have two reasons for this. First, a lot of guys are going to offer dinner and/or a movie for a first date with a girl. Remember that you want to be different from other guys and stand out! Second and most importantly, eating out actually lowers your odds most of the time. Don't get me wrong—if you know what you're doing and know how to work it, dinner is fine. In general, however, even after reading this book, it's going to lower your chances for understandable reasons. First, a hot girl who watches what she eats might just not want to have sex with you after eating a full meal (assuming she doesn't just have a salad). Second and more to the point, the blood in your body is going to be in your stomach digesting your food and will be less readily available to go to your penis and stay there when you need it. That, as you might imagine, is not good. Even if sex is not your goal on the first few dates, if you stuff yourselves you are probably going to feel a bit tired as your body is focused on digesting the food. This will limit the time amount of time and fun you spend out on the date. When it comes to the movies, unless she's a self-proclaimed movie buff and/or very interested in watching a movie, it can be boring and a bit awkward sitting in the dark with someone you don't know that well. Should you talk during the movie? If so, how much? Worse, will she talk too much during this movie that you really wanted to see? Again, both are okay if you know what you're doing.

In short, if you have to go the dinner and movie route, don't eat very much yourself. If she only eats a little, take it as a good thing. If you have to go to the movies to catch the latest film, be sure to talk about it before the movie and have something intelligent to say after the movie for the sake of conversation. Personally, because movies can be awkward, I find dinner is always a better bet and has better outcomes because you can interact more and use the act of eating to your advantage. More on that in chapter 12, the romance section of the book.

Museum or art gallery

These can be fun places to go if she's into art or history. You get to walk around, talk, and make insightful comments about what's on display. You also get to learn a little something about her: what moves her, what her taste in art is, and what she finds interesting. It's also inexpensive. Just remember you don't want to be right on top of her at all times. Let her go out ways from you, while you or her are looking at something, and let her return or pass by her while she's looking at something else. This way you don't come off as overbearing, which in her mind will equate to how you are in a relationship.

The zoo and/or botanical gardens

Animals are cool. You talk, you laugh, and you get to know each other's thoughts on the world, life, and that crazy, cute little monkey. You get to make comments and it's never quite the same each time you go. Flowers set up a nice fragrance and conversation and commentary is open to any subject.

Amusement parks, circus, and/or the rodeo

Here you get that free-spirited, I'm-a-kid-again feeling. No worries, no troubles, just fun and cotton candy. Just be sure not to eat and go on anything that's going to make you misplace what you just ate.

Conversational Ice Breakers

You're there, on the date at the place, or just picking her up, so now what? Icebreakers are just questions or comments designed to start the date and conversations. They are simple and something you do all the time. Here are a few of them you may want to use.

- So what did you do today?
- What do you like to watch on TV?
- What do you like to read?
- Do you like to go to the movies? What's your favorite kind of movie?
- Okay, I'm going to ask you a very important, possibly life changing, question. Are you a cat or a dog person?

You can also talk about current events in the news or pop culture. You can even talk about the surrounding environment. "Isn't this a nice little coffee shop?" Remember to keep your comments positive. You don't want her to think you're a whiner or someone who's never happy.

Above all, be sure to stay away from religious or political talk on the first date unless you meet at church, but even then keep the comments and speculations about God and the meaning of religion out of it. Such topics are taboo on your first few dates and can lead to arguments.

CHAPTER 11

How to Make Out and What Happens After

"God gave men both a penis and a brain, but unfortunately not
enough blood supply to run both at the same time."
~ Robin Williams

A Kiss to End All Kisses

Kissing is a game and it's a darn good one. If you are going to
play the game it does help to be prepared. That means if you
have any intention of kissing the girl on the date, watch what you
eat. Brush your teeth before you go on the date and carry breath
mints in your pocket just in case. Nothing kills a first kiss like
nasty breath.

There are of course lots of ways to kiss and to make out. Soft
and slow and rough and burning with passion are the two ends of
the continuum, but what to do for that first oh-so-scary first kiss?

The common mistake is that you and/or she are both so
nervous that it can be a disaster with one or the other planting a
kiss like an NFL linebacker plants his opponent on the ground.
Translation: you go for the kiss and end up slobbering all over her
or making it an awkward kiss. How embarrassing.

Well, the good news is you're reading this and that means you're going to be light years ahead of most in the kissing department too. Another thought to help with your rejection concerns is that a woman will forgive an overly aggressive guy more readily than a passive guy who doesn't make a move. Why? Because at the very least, she might be flattered by how attracted you are to her. If you don't make a move, odds are good she will think you're not into her, possibly gay, and one way or the other she is less likely to give in to your charms and your request for a second date. Make a move, go for the kiss, and if it's a no-go just be respectful of it and say you respect her for it. You will earn points with her one way or the other.

There is something to be said for experience but I am going to share with you the best way to go about the kiss. I say *best* because it incorporates several elements that will sweep her off her feet, if not take her breath away or land you right smack dab in the middle of her heart.

Romance and passion are key. Your kiss conveys a message about who you are and what you're like. You can of course do as you like, but when to do it and how to do it are topic of foremost concern. This approach incorporates many styles of kissing and is practically foolproof. Finding the right moment to kiss is the tricky part and is best done when she's not expecting it. The element of surprise is a powerful force. You can kiss during the date or at its end. Typically you want that silence, that small moment between your last conversational words and the next conversation you could have started. That moment when perhaps she's standing at her door, fiddling with her keys. That moment when she's just sitting down next to you or putting your drink down on the table. That moment when you are both getting up to leave some place. Perhaps at that romantic moment in the movie you're attending.

In that moment, when you pick it, you say nothing and do one of the following, keeping in mind you can mix in a bit of both if you so wish.

Option one is quick and dirty. Just go in and kiss her. Simple, reasonably effective, and a complete surprise. Remember that the element of surprise often has a desirable effect. Surprise activates the body by sending signals of joy and anticipation to the brain, heightening arousal. Scaring them a bit with a "Boo!" has a similar effect, but it won't get you any points.

Some women are uptight about kissing, especially on the first date. The following is a safer way to go about it without risking offending them.

Option two is moving slowly but deliberately with intent. With your eyes on her, put down anything you may be holding, reach out with your hand, step/lean into her personal space and gently brush the back of your fingers though her hair from her bangs (or the hair at her ears if she has no bangs), tracing down the side of her face.

While doing this, it's not uncommon for an abused or skittish girl to pull back. If this happens, simply pull back yourself and look her in the eyes and with all the warmth and kindness you can tell her "don't worry I wasn't going to hit you, I would never hurt you." Your tone will be a determining factor of how she responds.

Continue as follows: hand back up or reaching out as if to hold her hand . . .

As you trace the outline of that side of her face with your fingers, from the ear to the chin, move in while simultaneously and very gently lifting her chin up. You're doing this because it creates a safe, sensual feeling and positions them into an ideal kissing pose (assuming she's shorter). At this point do not attack her with a big, slobbery, tongue-gouging kiss!

Start small. Think bird kisses. Your mouth should be shut or partly open to match hers. Kiss twice slowly (thus avoiding first date kiss slobber, nose bumping, or completely missing your mark and screwing up) then the judgment call comes into play.

If the girl's into you, she's going to kiss you back. She's going to be leaning in, and her hands might even be holding you close. The third kiss will naturally build up. Think of it like starting a small fire that soon turns into a roaring one. Before you know it, you may be steaming up the car windows, kissing your way down the hall, and—who knows?—eventually against the apartment hallway that leads into the bedroom.

On the other hand, if she is not apparently into it and pulls back, look into her eyes and count *one Mississippi, two Mississippi* in your head. This tells her that you're not an animal. It's up to her but without words. Before anything is said, go back in for that third kiss.

Completely optional: bring your hand down her shoulder, down her arm, and . . .

Do *not* place your hand on the small of her back. Avoid this move. It creates a sense of "now you can't escape." Rather, go down to her hand(s) and hold them.

Okay, you romantic you. Guess what? She only dreamed or read about being kissed like that, but what if it's too romantic and soft for her? Nice guys finish last after all. No problem. During that third kiss, the kissing is going to intensify and build. I recommend never sticking the tongue out unless she starts it. Remember not to gag her with it.

Now for the kinky bad-boy kiss. During the third kiss or at a time of your choosing (I recommend at the end of the third kiss or the fourth) you are going to show some aggressiveness. Lean in more on the kiss, let your hands do some walking (stay above the clothing for now), pull back, and gently bite/tug on her lower lip a bit.

Say something nice like, "Wow, you're a great kisser." Girls don't generally know and like to hear it. This also makes another kiss far more likely.

Now go make like a vampire and nibble and kiss her neck. You don't want to overdo the kissing. Variety, after all, is the spice of life.

At this point it's all you, bud. You going to call it a night or go back in there?

Don't worry, I'm not going to leave out the very human fear of being rejected. What if she doesn't want to kiss you? What if she doesn't kiss on the first date? Should you even try to kiss on the first date? All good questions. Truthfully, it is a risk and you have to use your own best judgment based on how she seems to be responding to you verbally and by using her body language (we covered this already remember). Let's be honest: the first kiss is still nerve-racking and it always a concern for women too. If you are just not sure, or you are just so shy, there is one good, safe way to "test the waters" so to speak. It is most effective in a movie theater or as a "magic trick." In a theater, it's simple. You just let her have the popcorn or drink on her side then at some point in the movie lean over into her personal space as if you were going to kiss her. If she pulls back just grab the drink/popcorn. She won't know what to think. Were you going to kiss her, and if not why not? It will mess with her head a bit but it will save you some of your pride and you can try again another time.

As a magic trick it works in virtually any setting. All you got to do is place a quarter in the palm of your hand using your pinky and index finger to conceal it. Move in and get close like you're going to kiss her. If she pulls back, just react like "What's wrong? I was going to do the old quarter out of your ear trick." Smile and show her the quarter.

Using tactics like the "movie and quarter" trick are for those guys who are just starting out and super shy and afraid of rejection. In time, when their confidence goes up and up, they will use these less often. Rejection of a first kiss is not really that big a deal; it's not the end of the world (some women don't kiss on the first date as a rule so they won't think badly of themselves) and it probably is not even the end of you seeing this person.

Going Back in for Something More

If you do get this kiss and likely will (after all, you're reading this book and completing the homework assignments, right?), you may want to go back in for more kissing and who knows what else. While necking or kissing, place your hands on her hips, your left hand going up *not* on her boob but just under it. Your right hand (assuming you're right-handed) is going to pull a very effective maneuver known as palming. I think it has something to do with playing cards originally . . . just kidding.

Here you're going to slide your hand down her leg and back up, sliding your hand into the palming position on the *outside* of her pants onto her vagina. Gently but firmly you're going to rock and press your hand against her.

If she stops you, that's okay; she's not ready. Hopefully you're being honest when you tell her you don't want to do anything she doesn't want to do. Resume kissing if she wants (don't ask just go for it) and/or back off completely. This tells her two things:

1) You can control yourself and be a gentleman so she's safe around you and you will only go as far as she wants.
2) You don't need it or her so badly that you have to try to talk your way into bed with her. The result is *you don't need her she needs you!* As you know by now, this message is critically important.

If things are still hot and heavy, palming is going to really turn her on, warm her up, and get that engine going. Women not only like, but often need foreplay. Palming works because you're pressing on the clitoris. Now with that other hand you go up her shirt and pull her bra up, not down. The underside of the breast is sensitive and you don't want any stray wires poking her and ruining the moment, do you? Take your thumb and run it on the underside of one breast. Don't go for the nipple just yet. Lightly lick and flick your tongue around it and on it and then bite it or pop it in your mouth and press it between your lips—this is a safe way to do it if you don't trust yourself or if you have sharp teeth. Not hard, you don't want to hurt her.

At this point, I need to remind you that you're a man so don't be shy—go for it. Think about it: you're kissing, you're making out, she's half naked. Have some guts, and go for it. Depending on what she's wearing, you will take charge and undue her pants. If you're all thumbs, give it a try and tell her to help you take them off (not recommended, but what are you going to do if you're too excited to do it yourself?). Pull her pants off and panties with them if you can, *or* slide your hand down her pants and put your two middle fingers inside her. Not all the way, just half at first, and as she gets into it then all the way. Do this for a few minutes.

Now at this point you have to figure out what you want to do. I guarantee that if you want to see this person again and have her speak very highly of you, you're better off performing oral sex on her. Some people just don't go for this for various reasons and I'm not going to try to persuade you one way or the other. At this point you have basically seen her naked. If you just want sex and nothing else, go for it. Odds are 95 percent in your favor.

If you don't mind going down south, once her pants are off here is how:

Get down at ground level so you're facing her vagina and using your hands you're going to use your pointer fingers and index fingers to open up and pull aside the walls that hide her clitoris. Once you see it, your pointer finger is going to slide up and out just a bit in order to press on the base of her clit. This will make it pop up more fully exposed. Now proceed to lick and play with it all you want and drive her insane. The hard part is getting her to hold still and not losing your grip, thus losing track of it. It helps to go online and actually see the vagina and understand what it is you're looking for before trying this. As a warning, some girls find directly stimulating the head of the clitoris painful. So you may find licking around it and off and on is better.

If you think you might want to see this girl again, you might want to buy the for-her-pleasure condoms by Trojan to possibly up your chances. The better you are in bed, the more likely she is going to want to see you again, but not always. She might just be after a fling. You never know another persons reasoning. Remember the better you do the first time around, the more likely you will see her again for the next round.

You can pick up lots of sex tricks from books and websites and I encourage you to do that. I am going to save you a bit of time however and give four tips that will last you a lifetime as far as your bedroom antics are concerned. First, my advice is never, ever allow yourself to be handcuffed or tied to the bed with both arms. Doing that may lead to being robbed, photographed, and or killed by a man-hating psycho. Second tip, darkness. Turn off the lights and/or use blindfolds. Not for you, for her. Turning off the lights and blindfolding your girl will actually heighten her bodily senses during sex. This means she will like it more and that means she will like you more. If she asks why, tell her. I doubt she will object to some safe experimentation, but if she does not want to, don't. If she's not into it, fine. Third, no blindfold? Use an empty pillow case, fold it a few times, and tie it. Fourth tip, and this is the big one, is tantric sex. *The Kama Sutra* is cool, but tantric sex is what you have to study. Get a book on it. Why? Well, if you can do it, you will last longer in bed. That's always going to earn you points. Mostly, however, if you do it right it will intensify the power of her orgasms dramatically (some texts claim up to 500 percent), earning you points. Nothing builds the ego up like spontaneously being called a sex god. This means that even if she has no interest in you romantically, the odds are pretty high you will be on her cell phone list for that late night "I'm feeling lonely call." Perhaps best of all, the odds are pretty good that word of your bedroom skills will spread. Then you get to sit back and enjoy the attention you get while other guys are left scratching their heads wondering what they are doing wrong.

How to Tell Where You Are in the Dating Relationship

Clear indications that a girl likes you are if she hits you playfully on the arm or reaches out to touch you in some sexual (not very likely) or nonsexual way (very likely) way. Also, if she calls you to "hang out" and/or plays with/touches her hair and fiddles with her keys at the door, you're dating.

What Is Dating?

Dating can be broken down into three main categories. It is important to note that there is no rule for how to progress from one stage to the other. I provide an outline for how you should think and expect things to go. Also, another important note is to never assume that just because you slept with someone on the first night or whatever that you are in a dating relationship of any kind. People are different and move from one stage to anther based on their personalities.

For instance, if a woman is needy she may feel the need to be around you as much as possible, even as much as seven days a week, and if this needy woman starts dating a needy man who is fine with it then they can be said to have jumped right into steady dating. This is fine, however it is often the case that someone is needier than the other and a balance must be struck and talked about in a nice manner. Telling the other person to back off or how she is smothering you will often result in an end to the relationship.

Casual dating

Unless both people agree to date exclusively, you're casual dating. Typically this means you spend one or two days out of every few weeks together and dating others is still permissible.

Dating

You're in this stage of dating if you are going out with and seeing the person a few days a week at least three out of the four weeks in any given month. This does not mean you're exclusive, but you don't have any desire to see other people. But you still may.

Steady dating

Both of you have talked about seeing one another exclusively and commit to seeing only one another. In today's world it is necessary to point out that you won't be sleeping with anyone else as well.

Men often equate sex with intimacy. Keep in mind, however, that this is not the case from the female perspective. Intimacy means getting to know one another, spending time together, and creating memories of and with one another.

Back to Reality

Now you're at her door. Perhaps you have kissed a little, perhaps not. Well, you could just say good-bye, but if you're in it for something more, and she has not invited you for a drink herself, you can always resort to the nightcap line that goes like so:

Line: Hey, how about I come in for a drink for a few minutes before I go?

This is an invitation for something more that she may take you up on but was too shy to ask, but it also lets her know that at some point you will be leaving. When that will be depends on how things go.

When to Say "I Love You"

I love you is a very tricky phrase that has different meanings for different people. You should have at least made out seven or more times before even thinking about saying this. Love, like friendship, has different levels and flavors to it. You love your mom, your country's flag, your dog, your favorite TV show, etc. So when you say "I love you" be sure you get the meaning across to them. Don't tell them you love them more than your dog. Tell them instead that it's getting harder every day for you to imagine what life was like before you met her or some variation of this. Then say "I love you."

This still doesn't get to the heart of the matter: when do you say it for the first time? You can say it any place, but a romantic setting is always best. As a rule of thumb, you don't say this until you have been going out for at least two to three months. The reason being is that love can be a big word for some people and using it in order to get what you want (sex) is just plain wrong. You will end up hurting her feelings and—who knows?—she could be a psycho and just may kill you for it. Women are fully capable of handling themselves and being with a guy without you having to drop the "I love you" bomb. So show them and this concept we call love some respect. Don't say it unless you mean it, however you mean it . . .

Remember that the statement "I love you" also implies another question: "Do you love me too?" If she doesn't say "I love you" back, it's not the end of the world. Perhaps she just needs more time. Some people take longer to fall in love than others; nothing is wrong with that. Perhaps she doesn't and will never love you. Maybe she is going to break up with you. Well, I got good news. The good news is that regardless of you saying, "I love you," she was going to break up with you at some point anyways. At least you know where you stand, how she feels, and as a bonus you won't be wasting your time, cash, and emotions on her anymore.

What If the Other Person Says It First?

What if you are out on a date and the other person suddenly drops the "I love you" comment on you? Some would say what I am about to tell you is just plain wrong. That it's dirty, sneaky, and underhanded, but again you have to look at these things as human nature. Like a little kid who wants in the cookie jar, you have two options. The first is to just say "I love you" back. The second is to make her work for it. If you give a kid a cookie, that kid may take a bit of it and toss the rest on the floor. If on the other hand the kid has to get the chair, haul it into the kitchen, climb up the chair, and finally get that cookie, what happens? That kid is going to eat the whole cookie and is far less likely to toss any part of it on the floor. Working for the cookie is so much more rewarding than just having a cookie handed to you. Why? Because more effort went into it. The same holds true for dating and when to say "I love you." The more work the girl puts into it, the more invested she will be in you. It is the underlying principle of the "I don't need you but you need me attitude" and why telling a girl *no* can be so effective. I call this "the cookie effect." Not only do people want what they can't have, but they are more appreciative of it when they have to work for "the cookie."

Now in a perfect world if someone says "I love you" and you feel the same way, you respond, "I love you too." Please recall I mentioned at the start of this book it is not a perfect world. You should *never* respond with "I love you too" if you don't feel that way. Discuss with her how deep in love she thinks she is and see if you're in the same place. If you want to see her again and have a long-lasting relationship with this person, then I recommend *not* saying "I love you too." How you do this varies, but essentially it goes like so:

Her: I love you.

You: Cool.

Or

You: I like you too.

Or

You: Ditto.

That last one's a bit tricky. It implies the feeling of love that may or may not be there for you.

Preferably, if you're not willing to risk hurting the person or it is obvious that you have hurt her with one of the above responses, and/or you are concerned that not saying "I love you" back might cost you the relationship, you can always respond truthfully. There is an art form on how to do it however. Here are a few tips.

Put *baby, sweetheart, honey,* etc. in your response to her. These words are terms of endearment that tell her you do have some level of feeling for her beyond friendship and acknowledge her feelings.

Here is an example of what you might want to say: "Thanks, baby. I feel I need to be honest with you. I really care about you and *want* to keep seeing you. I didn't know how you felt about me and now that I do, I want to keep seeing you, but I hope you can understand that I need a little more time because I was afraid to let myself feel that way about you."

This tells her (twice) you want to be with her and keep seeing her but just are not so in love with her just yet. When you do get there and say "I love you" to her, it's that much more meaningful. If you want, you can always add on, "I know I'm falling for you."

While we are around the topic of dealing with your emotions and other peoples' emotions, let's take a brief moment to go over how to date your friends. This is tricky—should you tell how you feel? You might risk the friendship but if you don't, you might lose out on the love of your life. You never know. She might feel that way too but because she is a woman and lives by society's standards she may feel too inhibited or too shy to say anything to you about it and assume that you will or should make the first move.

Life is a risk, buddy, and if you don't have the guts to take the risk you probably won't get the glory. If you have the guts to take the risk and want the glory, you might want to try this. Ask her to sit down some place when she has nothing else to do and say something like this:

"I want you to know that you're my friend and *I would never hurt you* on purpose. You know *I am a grown man and I can handle this no problem,* but I think I should be honest with you. You know you're my friend. It's just that I like you and I wanted to tell you that because if you don't feel that way about me then at least I know I gave it a shot. That way *I can keep on being your friend regardless.* If you do want to go out and see what happens, how about we go out Thursday night at six?"

I put some of those words in italics because those are the words that you might want to put the right tone of voice inflection on to emphasis them.

In this way you are telling her you are an adult, you can handle your budding feelings for her, and dismiss them if she doesn't feel that way about you, while still putting major value on your friendship. Admittedly this outpouring of truth and showing vulnerability is hard, but that's why you do this with someone you know, like, and have a friendship with.

CHAPTER 12

Romance

"You need never run out of romance even
if your wallet runs out of money."
~ David Linares

How to Be Romantic

Ah, romance. Just what is it and how is it achieved? In order to be romantic you need not give flowers or chocolates or plan some special event on some special day. Being romantic is something you can do at virtually any time or any place.

It's true what some women find romantic varies from one to another, but how they like to be treated is not really any different from you or me. What follows are some options for being romantic.

Prepare breakfast in bed.

It helps if you don't burn it, but it's more the thought that counts.

Join her in the shower.

Just be sure to let her have the majority of the hot water.

Write a note of love on the steamy bathroom mirror.

Write a love note and slip it in her purse.
You can also call or send an e-mail saying something simple like, "I love you" or "I can't stop thinking of you" or "Just thinking of you." Whatever you want to say, just be sure to keep it short and meaningful. Do not include any things you need her to pick up from the store or other thing that are off topic.

The magic mirror.
Women love to look at themselves in the mirror making this ideal because it implants a mental image in her head of the two of you, but even without the mirror it can be romantic . . . Hug her from behind gently.

Think of her.
Give her a small gift, something that shows you care about her and her needs. If she's stressed, buy scented candles or massage oils for that massage you're going to give her after dinner. Just make sure it's *not sex-based*. This means buying lingerie or panties is a no-no.

Special dates.
Try springing a surprise date on her at someplace romantic or recreate a special moment you once had. You can do this on a day she gets overly dressed up, or ask her to dress up because you're going someplace special, or just show up during her lunch hour at work. Just don't give away where you're going on your date. The element of surprise and thought you put in it is what's really important. Just be sure to take her someplace *she* will like, not the local sports bar that only you want to go to so you can watch the game.

The good old days.
Go some place and let her know you remember this is where you first meet, kissed, or knew she was the one for you. In psychology this is called classical conditioning.

Does she have favorite cologne she likes you to wear? Well, here is a sneaky tip for you. Every time you make love be sure to wear just a bit of that cologne. After three or four times she will pair that smell with the thoughts of making love to you. Any time you want sex, your odds of getting it go way up just by wearing that cologne. You can pair the scent of your cologne to other things such as a romantic night out, making her recall those special moments whenever you wear it. This tip is something a girl told me she does to men. So no, I don't feel bad about telling guys to use it too.

Movie sex.

Anytime any place where it's just the two of you, start kissing her neck, nibbling on her ear, and placing your hands on and all over her body. *Do not say a word.* If she tries to talk, just tell her, "Shhh," and if necessary place one finger gently up to her lips and say it again (if you just have to speak, tell her no talking), continue making love to her right then and there or on the way to the bedroom if that's what you want. That's how they do it in the movies.

Reverse psychology 101.

What if your romantic overture fails? If she just is not in the mood? Try this. Tell her don't worry, you were not after anything, you just wanted to take a moment to show her how you feel about her. How sweet and romantic . . . she may be turned on and go for you right there or at the very least you can think of this as "money in the bank."

Taking the lead.

A night out dancing can be romantic, but what taking the lead really means is telling her what you want sexually. Don't tell her you want her on her knees or fantasize about joining the mile-high club. You're trying to be romantic, remember? Tell her *you want* to give *her* the best sex of her life. Tell her *you want* to give her the night of *her life* and the biggest orgasm she's ever had. Be concerned with what she wants and enjoys. Just be sure to be open to taking her lead and instructions in bed. As a bonus you can learn a lot about what she wants and what women like.

Standard compliments.

All women like to be told how beautiful they are. Remember when I mentioned memorizing a few poetry lines? You can use them here. Remember they don't have to be "flowery" and sound like Shakespeare; use what you like and can be sincere about it. "You're a ray of sunshine on a dark day, baby" or "You're so beautiful, your eyes are like sparkling stars in the night sky." Standard compliments can be as basic as "You look great." Nothing to it, right? You can make up your own.

Even the most beautiful girl likes to hear how beautiful she is, but the more beautiful she is, the less you should do it. Beauty is a paradox in that it's a great blessing and a terrible curse. How would you like it if people worshiped you for your looks and stared at you all the time but never once gave a damn about what your thoughts or opinions are? That would suck.

So be romantic and be sure to ask her what she thinks and let her tell you in full. Remember your conversational skills here.

Finding the weak spot.

Ever play one of those games where you have to remove some part of a structure like a straw or a block without having the whole thing fall down on you? This is the same tactic, only in reverse. Here you indulge her every wish or deepest one. Does she like chocolate? You don't have to go out and buy a whole box of them, just one single piece will do. What you're doing is tempting her and weakening her level of resistance and guess what? She will thank you for it too.

The environment.

Speaking of indulgence and weakening her resistance, what's around you is also important when being romantic. Presenting a box of chocolates at the subway while waiting for the train, not so romantic. Presenting a single piece of chocolate in a cozy, poorly lit cafe as you sit in a corner booth is much more likely to be effective. Another aspect of the environment to watch out for is tables. When being romantic, sit close to her and not across the table. The same thing applies to your home when you're trying to be romantic. Also keep the five senses in mind to spice up the environment.

The tease.

You recall the tease maneuver earlier on where you go for a drink placed on the other side of her seeming as if you planned on kissing her, only to get the drink or popcorn and pull back? Well, don't worry about kissing her at all. This works for romance too. In the right environment, it builds anticipation and anticipation is key.

Sex as play.

Anticipation maybe one important key, but it's the key to another more fun venue for adults called sex. There's nothing wrong with making a funny comment or asking for something you want in the bedroom. Just be sure you don't say something funny or mean about her. That will kill it.

Spontaneity.

What is it and how to do it? Being spontaneous or looking like it is not that hard. What is spontaneity in any kind of relationship in dating or even in marriage? It's showing the other person that you care and want to spend time with her or him, *doing something out of the day-to-day norm.*

- Showing up for no reason with flowers at her work, spontaneous and romantic.
- Buying tickets without her knowing for a weekend getaway where it's just the two of you and no one else is romantic. Unless they are for a golfing resort and she hates golf.

- Getting up off the couch all of a sudden with a fresh idea keeps things interesting: "You know what? Let's go for a drive" or "Let's go out and have some fun. What do you want to do?"
- Running through the sprinklers for no particular reason together and then taking a photo to remember how wet you two got: fun, goofy, and romantic.

See, it's easy. You just have to do something out of the norm that you can both enjoy.

Love and raindrops.

I honestly don't know why exactly—perhaps because it's in a lot of movies—but kissing in the rain is a huge, and I mean *huge*, turn-on for ladies and is very super romantic.

So long as you have an umbrella, it doesn't matter what kind of rain or snowfall you want to kiss in. If you don't have an umbrella you want to be sure to kiss during a warm summer rain or soft, lightly falling snow. No one wants to stand out in the cold being pelted by freezing rain or snow while you try to be romantic. So watch the weather.

Then there is always the *normal* way to go about romance. Put in a lot of effort to make the night as memorable as possible. A good way to think of this is what would you do if you were going to propose? Naturally you don't want to propose unless you want to get married, but that kind of night out on the town makes for a memorable date. This kind of effort should only be put out after the fifth date. If you do something too overt and romantic before she gets to know and bond with you, odds are you're going to come off as too intense for her.

Privacy.

Common sense should tell you that most people are not going to open up to you in a crowded room where everyone including her mother could possibly hear or see what the two of you are up to. For this reason, in order to create intimacy and privacy wherever you go and whatever you do, be on the lookout for those little places, those niches in the room, and those corner booths. Slip out of the party and go for a stroll or, even better, a moonlit stroll. (Say *stroll* when you ask; the word *walk* doesn't have the same effect.) The point is that throughout the day, whatever you're doing, you can have the opportunity to talk and connect even if it's only for a minute.

Valentine's Day.

There's no way around it: you need a gift and a nice one. If you haven't been dating that long, flowers, candy, dinner, and one of the aforementioned places to go out on a date are all fine. If you have been together longer than eight months, get out the wallet because you're going to need to buy a real gift. Hard to go wrong with a diamond. Just keep it (the diamond) and your gift small, at least for the first few years.

Homework Assignment 6

Homework: This is a repeat of your first homework assignment. Go out again to a place of your choosing and ask out (using the skills you have learned) ten people and keep track of how many of them said *yes*. Remember you are asking for a date and not sex, at least not yet; remember one thing at a time.

The point of this exercise is to determine your new level of functioning. During each attempt you should note what difficulty, if any, you are having talking to women. The reason being is that it will help you and tell you what it is you most need to improve on and review. Additionally, this will provide you with a real tangible gauge on how well your dating skills are currently, and how much they have improved at this point. You may need to do this two or three times to get an average because if you just do it ten times then you can psyche yourself out by adding too much mental pressure.

CHAPTER 13

Cheating

"It is better to suffer wrong than to do it, and happier to be
sometimes cheated than not to trust."
~ Samuel Johnson

Identifying a Cheater

Cheating is a deep emotional concern for anyone looking to
be in, or who is in, a relationship. I realize the book is not
called *Relationship Basics 101,* but I include cheating in this book
because once the dating gets serious, a relationship can happen but
you need to be careful. Cheating can only take place at the stage
of steady dating as defined in this book. This chapter addresses
how to spot and identify a potential cheater before you reach that
stage of commitment of steady dating as well as how to determine
if you're being cheated on in your established relationship.

The cheater's mind

There are many reasons why someone, perhaps even you,
might cheat on someone. Perhaps the cheater believes that "the
grass is greener on the other side of the fence" and goes out seeking
to find someone better. It could be that he or she was cheated on
by an ex and fears you cheating and cheats on you because she

thinks you will do it! It could be that knowing she has someone who cares for her makes her feel more confident and she may want to explore the possibility of others feeling about her as you do. In short, you provide an ego boost that makes her feel good enough about herself to go cheat!

Perhaps she saw how her mom or dad was treated in their relationships and as a result follows that same self-destructive pattern. It's possible that the cheater is just never satisfied and seeks more love and attention than what would be seen as normal, so he or she gets this love and attention from others. Make no mistake about it: you can be cheated on physically as well as emotionally. Both lead to breakups. The possibilities as to why people cheat are nearly endless and tie in to the person's past and psychological state of mind. Trying to understand why someone cheats is a waste of time and effort. It is by far more productive to sniff out potential cheaters before becoming too romantically involved.

There are some common sense signs that you might have a cheater on your hands. Examples might be her jumping into the shower the second she comes home or the smell of another mans cologne on her. These could mean she has been a little to close to another man for your liking. Short of these everyday signs, the potential cheater is likely to be described as:

1) Unable to hold down a job for longer than a year. Naturally one or two past jobs that ended before a year is fine for whatever reason, but when the pattern of unemployment is told to you or evident, it increases the probability that she has a cheater's mentality. After all, if she can't hold down a job and commit to showing up to work day in and day out, she may find it difficult to commit to you and to stay with you during the hard times.

2) The cheater is likely to be someone who insists you pay more than your fair share of the date or bills. It may seem callus, but the investment of time and money are indicators that she is more likely to be invested in a one-on-one relationship. Additionally, once you can no longer

afford to keep her she will seek greener pastures with someone else that can.

3) The cheater is often away from the home normally, claiming to have to work late and often for periods of time longer than a month.

4) The potential cheater also abuses drugs and alcohol. Yes, this includes such seemingly harmless and in some circles socially acceptable drugs like marijuana. The reason being is that any drug that is abused (used more than for rare recreational purposes) is taken to enhance the pleasurable sensations and feelings we have. Sex and drugs practically go hand in hand. The danger then is that while in this altered mood state people may have sex with another person. Even if they don't, there is still the danger that the very presence or repeated presence of another person while in this state of impaired judgment and mind can cause a mental paring between that guy/girl they are always getting high with and those good times feeling they are sharing. In short, it's a feeling she is not having with you. This does not mean you should be doing drugs with her. Honestly, you can't be there every time anyhow. The danger in dating this type of person naturally extends even further into the danger of contracting a sexually transmitted disease.

5) Another trait of a potential cheater is someone who is not close to her family, particularly the mother or a mother-like figure. The general reason is that if she does not have a female role model that she respected growing up, she is less likely to act like a lady in a relationship.

6) The cheater is highly reluctant to accept blame or take responsibility for anything less than the ideal and lies over little things. Typically cheaters blame not only other people for their problems but more often their partners in order to gain the power of guilt over the relationship. In this manner they not only gain power and control over the relationship but also *justify* their cheating to their partner

and themselves. Once the cheater is busted for cheating, it is common to hear her or him claim that she or he only cheated because the partner was never home, the partner never does anything for her or him, etc . . .

7) If your partner is constantly short on money and has not been so before, she may be spending that money on someone else.

8) Talk to your partner and if it looks like she has a poor mentality about sex (meaning she describe sex as "just being sex"), that is a good warning sign too. Many cheaters do not understand that, STD risks aside, sex can be equated with intimacy (most people refer to intimate sex as love making). This is why you often hear a cheater claim, "It was just sex, but I love you." Put in another way, if it barks like a dog and a walks like a dog, it's a good bet it is a dog, and the definition of a female dog is a *bitch*.

9) She accuses you of cheating. On the one hand it could be she has been cheated on in the past and is just insecure because of that. On the other, it could be she is feeling guilty about cheating and hoping you are too so she doesn't have to feel bad about it so much. You have to know about her history to find out.

10) She is secretive over her texts and emails and defensive about where she has been. This is never a good sign. It may just be she is cheating.

It is important to note that not one of the ten signs guarantees you have a cheater on your hands, only that the potential for them to cheat on you is there. Four or more of these signs increases the probability that you do or will have a cheater on your hands.

Note however that any one of the ten I mentioned generally leads to poor-quality and short-lived relationships regardless of you being cheated on or not.

The question of what to do if you think you're being cheated on is a point of argument for people. Some people claim that without complete trust you can't love completely. You should essentially trust your partner and if things don't work out and he or she wants to leave, that's fine. That's the risk you take when you have relationships. In other words, is the risk of being hurt worth the price of love? If you say *yes,* then you must trust 100 percent.

Others claim that if you suspect cheating or any problem in your relationship that you should sit your partner down and talk to them about it, that it could just be your insecurities and not that your partner is doing anything wrong. Talking out your problems with your partner does have many benefits, but let's be honest: if your partner is cheating on you, she is likely to lie to your face and do whatever you say in order to throw you off the trail.

Finally, there are those who believe that *the proof is in the pudding,* meaning that they want to know without a shadow of a doubt that their partner is being faithful. Such people may seem low on the personal trust side of their relationship and hire detectives or, knowing their partner's schedule, follow her or him around. Another way to look at is that the person doing the following is deeply in love and concerned about the relationship and the possibility of being hurt. If such a person were to find out that she was indeed working late and not cheating, this would enhance the level of love and commitment in the relationship thus potentially removing the person's nagging doubts and fears.

If you are of the mind to follow this third line of thought it is important that you take a friend with you on your little surveillance trip not only for your safety but to keep you from doing anything stupid if indeed you find you are being cheated on.

Use good judgment and, depending on your partner's day-to-day schedule, follow her as long and often as you see fit, but do not exceed more than two weeks consecutive time. If she is cheating on you it will likely become evident to you sometime during those two weeks. By *follow* I mean only if you see her going someplace other than home, typically after working hours. It should be sufficient otherwise to simply confirm where she is by driving past her work or mother's house if that's where she says she is going to be and verifying that she is where she says s/he is. This takes very little time.

I do not suggest that you stalk them, sitting in your car for hours at a time or secretly scrutinizing their every move and bank account records (perhaps she's buying you a gift). Such overdone and obsessive behavior shows a deep flaw not in them or your relationship but within yourself! Remember there is a difference between checking on the status of your relationship and stalking it. Ideally you should be able to trust.

When you really look at cheating and your suspicions, it probably says more about you than your partner. I have always found the person who is afraid of being cheated on has cheated or has been cheated on in the past. If that is you, I advise you to seek counseling and do your best not to let your fear ruin what may well be a good start to a beautiful relationship. You can be sure to expect more on this subject in my next book.

CHAPTER 14

Specialty Topics of Interest

"Guessing is cheap; guessing wrong is expensive."
~ Chinese proverb

Random Thoughts and Observations

This chapter is for information that didn't quite fit in other chapters or would have taken away from the main point of other chapters, but it's still really important if you want to avoid dating embarrassment. The information here is mostly for those people who are looking to round out their understanding of dating and their basic skills.

After the First Date

At the end of the first date, you should invite her out for the second date or wait no more than one day and invite her out for a second date via phone or in person. This creates a whirlwind romance effect and it keeps the sense of excitement alive. Sometime in the first date you need to ask what her ideal date is or what fun activity she likes to do. That's going to be your lead-in for the second date. At the first date's end, just offer to go do what she stated or something like that. If you just plain forgot to ask what she is into or can not recall her saying anything she likes to do on the date just ask what she would like to do for the second date.

After the Second Date

Once you have the second date out of the way, you need to set up the third. The third date should be an *activity date.* That means dinner and movie are not options. Do something that causes her to picture the two of you as a couple. Just be sure to remember that going out to dinner and bowling or a movie every time gets old. Be sure to mix up your activity dates.

Conversation Side Rules

Conversation doesn't mean you have to agree with everything she says. In fact, as a rule you shouldn't. If you do agree with everything she says, you will probably be seen as boring. She may also see you as being too nice and possibly trying to hard. Challenge her mind and make her think about what she is saying. Don't be afraid to briefly mention your own thoughts and opinions even if they are different from hers. This does not mean that you should try to make her feel stupid or make yourself look smarter than her. Simply asking for her to clarify her thoughts and opinions can do the job nicely.

Another rule of thumb is to compliment her mind. Tell her something along the lines of how you never thought of *it* that way before or that you can see her point of view. Doing these things enhances your chances of her feeling like she is bonding with you on an emotional as well as on an intellectual level. Remember the old saying that "when in debate, you and the point you are trying to make are two different things." If you don't agree that is okay. Try not to take it personally.

Also, a major rule when out on a date is not to check out other women! This takes serious training and mental awareness for most men. You just can't do it at all when starting to date a girl because she will look at that as a warning that you are already losing interest in her and so she will likely dump you as fast as she can. So be sure to stare at her right eye, the tip of her nose, or her lips when you're looking at her and do not let your eyes wander to other women.

Keep Your Place Clean

You don't want to be a neat freak because it makes you look obsessive and controlling, but you don't want your place to be a mess either. This means don't leave any dirty clothing or personal hygiene products lying about or scattered in your room. In the worst-case scenario, she walks out disgusted. Best-case, she lets you run inside and throw stuff in a closet corner. One way or the other you look like a pig, your place smells, and it makes you lose your cool. You want to be seen as cool. Last but not least, if you think your place is a hole in the wall with carpet stains and the occasional cockroach, hit the lights fast and light up a few scented candles. It will hide some of your home's more . . . interesting flaws, and girls will typically see this as a sweet show of effort on your part and will likely be more forgiving of your mess.

The Direct Approach; When Push Comes to Shove

It's possible to go the direct approach with a woman. No games, no smooth lines, but in all honesty ladies, just like men, appreciate a challenge. If you're not sure, watch and see how she interacts with others (waitress, ticket girl, whatever) and note if she smiles more at you or seems nicer to you. This might tell you something but if you're going to go this route no matter what and all else fails, you have to sell yourself. No, I am not referring to you becoming a male prostitute. What I'm talking about is how to make yourself so interesting and attractive that a woman would have to be nuts to take a pass on a great guy like you. Never just flatly say anything stupid like, "I like you, want to go out some time?" Yes, that can work, but you can also hit the lottery and become a millionaire tomorrow. Instead, with confidence and your tone of voice say this:

> Hi, I'm (your name). Look, this is kind of odd I know, but have you ever seen someone and just felt a connection of some kind like a recognition? Maybe you're walking down a street and your eyes meet with someone just for a moment (now would be a good time to look into her eyes) and then they disappear. Maybe that happens a few times in your life but if you don't act on it you will always wonder what if, just what if . . . And, well, I didn't want to have to wonder about that so I wanted to introduce myself.

Why does this work? Well, along with showing a lot of confidence to go up and say something like that and using your smooth tone of voice, this little baby works because you're playing on several human weak points. First, but not necessary foremost, you're playing on her curiosity. You are also planting a seed of doubt in her mind that if she turns you down she could be missing out on "the one." Now I ask you: what girl doesn't want to find that special someone? Your pitch will sell her on the idea of giving you a chance.

Regret

A possible positive to being rejected is that you will probably get some respect from the other guys in the place for having the guts to go for it. All men know and have been there at some point and time and recognize the balls it takes to make a move. At some point you are going to have to make a move and let your intentions be known. Even if a girl is all over you it is still necessary to respond somehow. If you don't, you risk living with the regret of never having at least tried. This is much worse than suffering a moment of rejection. Think about it and I know you will agree.

Crashing a Wedding

Fun, but not wise. Should only be attempted if you live in a huge city like New York. You risk social humiliation and that's really bad if you run into someone from the wedding down the road in life. You often have to lie while there, and that's not a good way to start a relationship if you end up falling for someone you meet. In some cases, you might even be arrested for trespassing. Still, I won't lie: it's a great place to meet women and really ups your chances on getting laid as well as in a relationship. Best way to go to weddings is to have lots of friends and get invited to one.

Never Tell a Woman What Not to Eat

Unless you want to piss the girl off, *never ever* order for the girl on the first few dates (*if ever*). It will be seen as controlling. Only recommend what you think is good at the place you're eating at and nothing more. No matter what—unless you want to risk death—you should never tell her not to eat anything unhealthy. Girls know what's healthy and what's not (probably more so than you) and your telling them will accomplish two things. First, it will make you look like a control freak. Second, it will give the impression you're just interested in her body. Both will take you out of the running.

Putting Yourself in Their Shoes

One of the biggest reasons relationships don't work out is because someone in the relationship failed to take into account the other person's thoughts and feelings. This is the thing that seems to causes more confusion and ends more relationships than perhaps any other. Relationships and why they work or fail is a deeply complex issue that looks at the personalities and interactions between people and is best sorted out by a professional therapist in person. What I'm going to tell you here is a simple story that showcases the most common mistakes made in relationships as I've see them.

Steve liked to park his car a block away from his girlfriend's house. He didn't really have a reason for it other than *"just because"* when his girlfriend asked him why he parked so far away. The relationship ended shortly thereafter. I use this story to point out common factors in a relationship. Steve felt that, as a man, he didn't have to explain or give any reason for parking his car so far away. The result was that his girlfriend felt cut off from him, like he was hiding something from her or possibly embarrassed to have his car (and by extension him) seen at her house. By refusing to do something as simple as explaining why, or just start parking in front of her house, he turned a minor thing into a huge problem. A relationship ended because he never thought to ask himself why she wanted him to park closer.

There are a few lessons that can be learned from Steve's story. The first is that in any relationship you have to pick and choose the right battles. Second, you must be willing to talk to the other person in the relationship when he or she has an issue that is clearly bothering him or her (when he or she brings it up a few times is a hint even if they don't seem upset). Third, don't let your ego get in the way.

There are three questions that if you ask yourself at least once a month will increase the chances of your relationship lasting dramatically. The first is *What might I be doing to upset my significant other?* It's a hard question to ask and answer because sometimes we just don't see what it is that we're doing wrong. Often this is because we fail to take the other person's thoughts and feelings into account. The very nature of a relationship is to often take the other person's thoughts and feelings into account and stop thinking of just yourself and stop acting solely *on your own all the time.* If you can't think of what you may be doing to upset your significant other then ask yourself *What is it I can do to make my significant other happier?*

The third question is one you ask your girlfriend (when you are steady dating). You start by asking her what she thinks and/

or feels about something you do or want to do. It is not a sign of weakness to do this; in fact, it is a sign of strength. Asking these questions means you are man enough to hear what she has to say, not that you're afraid to be real with her and ask. Take what she says under advisement. This does not mean you're obligated to do what she says or agree with what she thinks, it just means that you at least respected her and cared enough about her to ask and listen to her. That is mainly what a woman wants and if you can do these few things even at a bare minimum of once a month you will dramatically improve your relationship and the chances of it lasting a long time.

Asking and acting on these questions doesn't erase everything you learned before, particularly about saying *no* and conveying a "You need me, I don't need you" attitude. This only means that once you are in a dating relationship you need to be smart enough to use them in moderation. In truth, during long dating relationship these opportunities will come up naturally. This means you don't necessarily have to say *no* to something just to make a point or over something that could be important to her and your relationship.

Movie Lines

There is an almost limitless number of catchy lines and romantic acts that a guy can do to impress and get the girl. So many that it would take several books much longer than this one in order to get a lot of the good ones down on paper. That means you are pretty much screwed because you can't possibly remember them all. Instead, try something like this: when you see a movie or read a book with a romantic scene or line that you like, write it down and put it away someplace safe. Wait about a year and a half to two years (long enough for most people to forget it and the movie/book it came from) and then you can use it. It's a great trick, works well, and even if your girl recognizes the line she has no way of knowing that you got it from a movie or book but it will conjure up that romantic feeling that she had with the book or movie.

Compatibility

One of the interesting things I have observed so far in couples is the apparent mismatch between highly affectionate people, who come from very loving and expressive families, and those who do not come from very loving or very emotionally expressive families. You might think that highly expressive, emotional people would tend to couple up with other highly expressive emotional people, but it seem more often the opposite is true. I only include this thought here because it may be useful to observe in the person you're dating how emotionally expressive she is in relation to how you are. It's not always the case however.

Drugs

If you're on any kind of illegal drug, you're not fit to date. Period. Drugs take away time from life and twist who you are as a person. Drugs are done in an attempt to cope with painful emotions and memories. Get help. Never date or expect to have a successful dating relationship with a woman who uses drugs for the same reasons. In today's world, everyone knows drugs are bad for the mind as well as the body. If a woman uses drugs it means she does not respect herself and that means she will not respect you.

How You Look

This topic I really struggled with even mentioning because I was concerned that some might think it's counter to what I said early in this book about being yourself and not having to dress or act a certain way to get a woman. This is still true and I cannot stress this enough. You don't need someone to tell you to get in better shape and all that. This is not what I am going to talk about.

You see, on one hand you are not how you dress or how you look. The you that is you is something very personal and deep within you. Some might call it your *soul* while others call it your *personality.* Whatever you call it, I want to say to you that this book and the following won't or shouldn't change that at all. These are just some things I think you should be aware of. That is it, I just want you to just be aware of these things and do what you think is best for yourself and what works for you. I'm not going to go into how to dress or much of anything else really. I just want to point out a few basic things that women typically notice about a guy.

First is the hair. What does your hair say about you, and is that the message you want to give people? Example: what does a Mohawk hair cut make you think? Does the cut of your hair match that shape of your face? If you are not sure, suck it up and go to a salon and have one of those cute hairstylists cut your hair. It is their job to make you look good and as a girl she will cut your hair to make you look good. Then go back to your barber if you want.

If you have glasses think about getting contacts. Yes, glasses make you look smarter and even more sophisticated (and that can work in certain situations and environments), but in the popular culture's mind they are still equated with being a thing for nerds and geeks or at best for dorks. Stereotyping is wrong but that's how it is in most people's minds. When you do wear glasses, make sure to get a pair that makes you look good and fits the shape of your face. Ask a female friend to go with you when picking out a pair if you have to or just ask the person (preferably a girl) selling them.

Finally, there are your shoes. The brand doesn't matter because, like I said, if a girl is going to be so shallow as to date you based off what you're wearing, she's not worth it. I just point out the shoes because typically a woman is going to look at your shoes. Women like shoes, and in some way judge you by how nice and new your shoes look. So if you have old shoes that look ragged and worn out, you may want to pick up a new pair.

Respect

Respect. Jerks and bad boys often get away with treating a girl badly but my own observations have revealed that almost all of them show some degree of respect in the following ways (if not in public then when they think they are alone, or it's just me their friend who is *secretly* observing them). The guy can cuss but not cuss at her. Even cussing is almost always not okay because people tend to think you're cussing at them, even when you think it's obvious you're not and only cussing at the situation or the dumb guy who cut you off. Know how to eat in a high-class restaurant if you don't you come off as crude. Know at least the basics about flowers and in particular her favorite flower, and that a red rose is for love and passion. That way if you ever need to buy her some you know. Always hold the door open for her. Stop smoking. Even if she smokes, you need to stop. Respect her lungs even if she does not. Besides, even if she is okay with you smoking, it is not attractive to see someone cough up a lung and smell like ash.

Tips for Meeting the Parents

If you ever get to that point of meeting the parents (typically this means you are on the verge of a long-term relationship), it can make or break you and that girl you are dating. True, she could say to heck with what her family thinks of you, but when both you and she are looking for a more committed relationship and want to take things to the next level, it is really hard to ignore the opinions and wishes of nagging parents.

Meeting your girlfriend's parents for the first time is going to be nerve-racking. Accept it as a natural inevitability. The good news is that most parents will want to like you and even if they don't, feel happy that you got this book. What follows are some very useful tips to make that first impression a good one.

1. First impressions count.

Looking good is critical. You don't want to overdo it and look like a player, but you don't want to go over in sweatpants and a T-shirt. This means don't have a ball cap on, cartoon T-shirts or really baggie clothing. I recommend dress pants (jeans if you don't have dress pants), tennis shoes, and perhaps a dress shirt or T-shirt untucked. Why untucked? Tucking in the shirt often gives the impression you're uptight, restricted, and a serious "business" ready kind of guy. That would be okay in an office but you're meeting her parents. Plus, dressing average or for the occasion will make sure you are not caught unprepared for any family events they might have. Imagine being all decked out and asked to play some football with her dad and brothers out back. Grooming and presentation count when meeting the parents. With that being said, it doesn't mean you need to be a male model to wow the parents, but you do need to take more time than normal to impress. This means be sure you don't have dirt under your nails. File your nails a bit, trim your nose hairs, and wax your ears. Believe me: most moms are going to look at the finer details of how you look. To make it worse, most moms will read into those smaller details as well.

2. Get information on them.

If you need to ask your girlfriend do so, but you will want to know any cultural customs they have: religious values, languages, hobbies, and interests. Language is a specialty issue and if it is different from your own, learn how to pronounce basic greetings without error. Preparation is vital, especially if you are meeting the parents during a holiday season and the way they celebrate is different from your own.

3. Know what names to use when meeting the parents.

Using the family's last name when meeting the parents is very polite and has a hidden benefit for you. It could be that they are just polite and don't mind you calling them by their first names, but after a while if they ask you to call them by their first names it is an indication they like you.

4. Bring a gift.

No matter what, when meeting the parents for the first time don't go empty-handed. The research you do in tip number two will come in handy when figuring out what to bring. Flowers, a certain wine, or some homemade food may or may not be appropriate, but you'll never know unless you ask. Unless it is culturally inappropriate to bring a gift, bring one. Period.

5. Avoid touchy topics.

This tip needs to be stated clearly. Avoid all taboo topics. This includes anything currently in the news that could be debated: politics, sex, religion, and even sports. The *only* time to break this rule is if you are 100 percent sure that you and the parents agree on the subject. Even then don't go crazy on stating your opinion(s). You are probably being tested (most likely by her mother) and that's okay and understandable. So keep this in mind.

6. Manners count.

This means you must offer to help (mostly with mom) in setting the table and doing the dishes. You're a guest and a good guest tries to show the proper amount of appreciation. Be sure to say *please* and *thank you,* and avoid using slang or casual terms like *cool* or *yep.* Also, treat annoying and/or frustrating family members (including pets) with kindness. You would be surprised at how often it is a test. If not a planned test, other family members probably know how annoying that family member can be and will applaud your kindness.

7. Be the best you can be.

This last tip may seem odd given the other tips, but remember the you that is you is more than how you behave. Keep in mind this is a first time deal. Little by little you can let your defenses down and feel more at ease around the parents. Think of it as an opportunity to put your best face forward. Show who you are, stand proud, and don't apologize for your thoughts or opinions if you are busted saying or doing something that offends them. Saying you're sorry if the parents disagree is fine. My point is if something does go astray, be polite but okay with it and they will be more okay with it too. Your girl's parents will likely appreciate you for how kind but firm you can be and in turn see why their girl fell for you, and even how you can be good for her.

Confidence over Arrogance

I wanted to add this in at this point as a specialty topic about the philosophy of this book and so it would be one of the last things you read. That way it is more likely to stick in your mind (it's called in psychological terms *the recency effect)*. A warning to one possible unforeseen danger of this book is to watch how cocky you get. Yes, you are a stud by knowing the basics and ahead of most guys. Still, I have run across several guys who are so obnoxious that their confidence sours and turns to arrogance. This happens for lots of reasons and most can be addressed and fixed with a little insight, some friendly advice, or a bit of counseling. Keep this thought in mind when you get to feeling too good about yourself: A humble but confident man will get a lot more feminine attention than an arrogant or conceited one will.

This is particularly important when it comes to being successful in a long-term relationship. An example is my friend "Bill". My friend Bill started off as a nice but dorky guy who managed to get some female attention. Typically it was not from the kind of girls he would have preferred, but in his mind something was better than nothing. Bill got an unpublished draft of my book that I had given him and I was so proud of him. He really took off dating the kind of attractive, sexy girls he had always wanted. Then something happened. It seems that Bill got his heart broken and to deal with the pain he started listening to the advice of another friend who appealed to his ego. This friend did for Bill what a lot of other books do for men. He *built up his ego* by saying *he could get another girl, there were plenty of fish in the sea, fuck 'em all, you're the man, girls should bow down to us as men,* etc.

This kind of "I am the king and better than everyone else" talk appealed to Bill and the result was really bad. I did some investigating and it turned out that his ex didn't even dump him; she moved out of the state and that ended the relationship. Bill should have taken the time to reflect on why the relationship ended, to have grieved the loss of the relationship, and to have healed his emotional wounds. This may sound very touchy-feely to most men, but that's what we as human beings need to do to deal with the emotional baggage. He did none of this. He pushed the pain down and just moved on to sleeping with the next girl and the next girl.

Very quickly Bill stopped following the guidelines of this book because his attitude toward women and how he saw himself changed. Now Bill is so arrogant and repulsive to most women that he almost never gets a date. Word of his attitude problem has spread in the town. On top of this he completely lost touch with the philosophy and teaching of this book. Sadly, arrogance is attractive to some women, but typically not the mentally healthy and physically attractive *majority.*

I want to again impress on you as a reader that your attitude is the most important aspect of your communications with women. If you start thinking you are the king and so much better than everyone else, you are setting yourself up for a very hard fall. Truth to tell, Bill's arrogance and rep are so bad most *men and women* don't want to be associated with him.

To avoid becoming like Bill, I recommend sticking to the basic philosophy of this book and to recognize that no matter how great a person you are, no matter how often you score, you're still only human. This means you are still going to suffer like everyone does, not only in your life but in your search for sex and/or love. Accept it, deal with it, and you will successfully move on with your goals. Otherwise you risk spending years of your life like Bill: alone, desperate, and confused about what it is you're doing wrong.

White Knight Syndrome

White Knight Syndrome is an unofficial cultural diagnosis for men who are always trying to save, rescue or make excuses for women. In this book I gave dozens of possible reasons that a guy might get rejected at no fault of his. Yet if a guy is not carful he may use those possibilities as an excuse to keep trying get a girl or to put up with poor behavior from his love interest. Essentially that makes him a stalker or a door mat. In one case or the other he is not going to get the girl because she won't respect him. Remember she needs you. I hope you my reader won't develop this issue. If you suffer from it do your best to stop. Recognize that everyone deserves to make mistakes so they can learn from them in this journey we call life. You don't need to save her from whatever mistake she is making. You don't need to save her from her family or her friends. She has to live her own life and make her own choices. The best you can do is offer her a choice, like dating you. If she screws it up that is her fault. Stop trying to control her or cover for her. In the end it is about you and not wanting to feel hurt or let down. Deal with the pain and move on. It hurts less as you too move on in your life journey.

Exceptions to the Rule

You have now learned almost all of the basics that will apply to the vast majority of women. Keep in mind that people grow up with different lives and different personalities and want different things at different stages of their lives. For instance, when some women are young, they like guys who are really rough around the edges. I can't even tell you how often I was surprised to find a very attractive, sexy girl dating a complete loser with dirty clothing, worn-out shoes, no job and who spent his free time sleeping on her couch. Each time I asked these girls what they saw in these guys, it was always a mix of the guy's attitude, availability (the guy asked them out), and a personal flaw on the girls' part. I say a personal flaw because so many of them admitted that part of the appeal was in having the majority of the power in the relationship. Several years later most of these girls had learned that dating those kinds of guys was a waste of time and had changed their taste in men for the better.

The point of this little story is that the psychology of a person and what he or she wants in anything, particularly relationships, is different from person to person based on the person's history, personality, and age (where they are in life and/or maturity).

This is the final lesson of the book and something that sadly you can only learn by the experience and practice of talking to people. By using your conversational skills, with reflective thinking on who they are as a person and by reacting to how they respond to you, with your body language and your words you can subtly alter your approach and nudge the outcome into your favor.

CHAPTER 15

Putting It All Together

"A master of one's inner experiences is a master at life."
~ Unknown

Essay Exams

No true book of learning would be complete without some final test essay questions! These are just some questions for you to think about and, if you like, write on. Essays make you go back and rethink or reread what you learned so the knowledge will sink in at a deeper level. This way you can do some critical thinking, mental dress rehearsals, and mentally adjust to different and common situations.

Exam 1

Question 1

You just happen to be sitting at your favorite restaurant alone when you notice that your waitress is very attractive. Her wedding finger has no ring on it. She is 5'9" and about 140 pounds and has all her hair completely pulled back into a ponytail.

What might you be able to assume about this person and what pick-up strategy would you use to get her number?

Tip: A single ring on the weeding finger likely means she's not married. Wedding bands typically come in pairs. Also, even if there is a ring it could be an engagement ring or, better still, a promise ring. Sometimes it is even the case that women put a ring of some kind on their wedding finger to dissuade men from hitting on them. This information can be useful and give you the knowledge to just go for it.

Question 2

You have been introduced to an attractive new person by a friend at a party. How would you introduce yourself to this person and how would you show interest in what she's saying to you in the course of your conversation, using *only* your body language? Assume that your friend has no objections to you speaking to that person and has left momentarily.

Question 3

What is the single most important thing you can say to someone you're dating or in a relationship with from time to time and why?

Question 4

What are the key things to remember in active listening and effective communication? Example: Ask open-ended questions.

Name at least four things in all.

Question 5

Please describe for me your ideal date. This means what you would do on your ideal date, where you would go, what you would do, what you would say, and what *she* would say. Keep it PG-13 and try writing this one out, making it at least one-page long, double-spaced.

The End . . . Kind Of

Congratulations on your new life, buddy. By now if you have followed this book well I have no doubt you can date and are suitable material for ladies to want to be in a relationship with. What follows after this are some appendix lists that can help you break down all this information in this book step by step. I thought you could copy them and put them in your wallet if you needed to review something in the moments before an attempt.

So now you know the basics and a little bit more of what every guy should, but sadly often doesn't, know. Be sure to pick up my next book tentatively titled *Dating Basics 102: What Every Guy Should Know but Often Doesn't)*, followed by other series books by yours truly.

Now get out there and enjoy your life!

If you have any questions, comments, or stories that you would like to share, send them via e-mail to <u>davidlinares@aol.com</u>.

Appendix A

Recommended Subjects You Should Look Up

I prefer books to the Internet, but if you can't afford to buy books on these subjects check them out online.

Read up on the topics of:

- How to read body language;
- Tantric sex;
- *The Karma Sutra* and pleasure/erogenous zones on the female body.

Check out YouTube for videos on reflective listening and active listening.

Read your local newspaper at least once every two weeks, even if it's just an article or two on the front page.

Watch your local or national news on TV at least once every two weeks.

Watching or reading the news like this won't take more than a total of 30 minutes to an hour of your time, every two weeks. That's nothing.

Appendix B

Date Preparations

Make your place look good and reasonably clean. Hide clothing out of sight.

Have (preferably) unscented candles in your room just in case of a power outage.

Be sure you look the way you want to look. Wax your ears, cut your nose hairs if they stick out, brush your teeth, and bring a few mints or sticks of gum to insure you don't have bad breath.

Are your shoes and general style of dress saying what you want them to say?

Know where you are going and how to get there and have a full tank of gas in your car.

Don't forget your little surprise gift: origami paperwork or magic trick or whatever to use on the date.

Appendix C

Step by Step Short Guide to Asking Her Out

Here is an ultra-fast cheat sheet on how to ask her out.

Recall a confidence-boosting moment in your life that made you feel good.

Say, "Hi, my name is . . ."

Shake hands if she puts hers out; if not, skip it.

Use a line or be funny.

Ask a question (what's around town, what she's wearing, anything like that).

Ask an open-ended question (who, what, when, where, but *not* why).

Reflect back a feeling in the conversation.

Be positive/make a positive comment/s.

Ask for a fifteen-minute mini-date. If you get the date, ask for her number.

When time is up, tell her you know you just met and it is sudden buy you have to be going soon to meet some friends. Ask for her number, then leave.

Appendix D

Phone Guide

Your rate of speech and tone of voice are going to be important factors when making your first phone call. You want to do two things when calling: make going out with you sound *fun* and appeal to her curiosity.

First dates are best conducted Monday through Thursday.

You: Hey, how you doing?

Her: "Good, how are you?"

You: "I have some free time and wanted to get together, figure we can go out and have some *fun* (put the right inflection of tone in your voice on the word fun) and I have a surprise for you too. How about this Thursday night at seven?"

After asking, shut up, look at your watch, and count out three seconds. If there's no positive response, continue.

You: "Oh, and I promise that if you don't laugh at least half the time we are out I'll refund all your money." Pause one second and then say, "And come to think of it, since you don't have to spend any of your money, you have nothing to lose." Chuckle lightly.

Her: "That sounds great. What are we going to do?"

Pick at least one thing you're going to do and if you feel like it, offer to let her pick one thing she wants to do. Normally you don't do that, but I like to let her pick something that she will enjoy just to show I'm open-minded.

You: "Well, I thought we'd go . . ." Suggest wherever you want to go.

Her: "Sounds great. I'll see you at seven."

Now, there *is* the possibility that she won't want to go out with you because something else has come up or you didn't make yourself sound worthy enough of her time. Here is how to recover.

Her: "Well, that sounds okay but I have to go . . ." blah, blah, blah, or whatever she says that means she can't go out with you.

At this point, she could just let you go or make you a counteroffer. If she really *is* busy but wants to go out with you, she will make a counteroffer.

Her: "Oh, well, I can't at all this week but next Thursday night at eight would be okay."

Don't fall for this trap. Even if she were to make you a counteroffer for the next day, say *no!* Remember that saying *no* puts you in control and makes her want you that much more. Plus accepting makes you seem too easy, eager, and available.

You: "That sounds great but unfortunately I can't. I have some important stuff I need to do."

You can add on "for my family" if you think it will score you points. It depends on the girl.

You: "How about we do Thursday at five instead?"

Or

You: "How about we do Monday instead, say six o'clock?"

Her: "That will work. I'll see you then. You can pick me up at . . ."

When the timing is off and you can't work out a date reasonably quickly, there are essentially two options.

1. Tell her that you will try again when her schedule's not so busy. The hidden meaning is she being too uptight about this. A date is just a date after all. It's not like you're asking for a lifetime commitment.

2. Tell her, "Well, this is just how I like to do things when I call or make a date with someone and something has come up. I leave it up to her to call and make the next date. If you want to go out, I am interested. Call me."